IF THE
FOUNDATIONS
BE DESTROYED

Chick Salliby

Salvation message at conclusion by
Maureen Salliby

Word and Prayer Ministries
P. O. Box 361
Fiskdale, MA 01518-0361

Copyright © 1994 by
Rev. Charles Salliby

ALL RIGHTS RESERVED

Scripture quotations marked (NIV) are taken from the HOLY BIBLE, NEW INTERNATIONAL VERSION®. NIV®. Copyright © 1973, 1978, 1984 by International Bible Society. Used by permission of Zondervan Publishing House. All rights reserved.

Library of Congress
Catalog Card Number 94-90335

13th Printing

Printed in the United States of America
By Faith Printing Company, Taylors, SC

DEDICATION

To my wife Maureen, who is also my dearest friend. Her life in Christ has been my greatest inspiration and challenge over the years. Her unfailing support and assistance in the ministry, including the many hours she has contributed to this book, has also made her my helpmate in the purest sense of the word.

To our wonderful children, their spouses, and children, without which life for both Maureen and I would never be the same.

To Rev. Francis King, his wife, and congregation who have paid dearly for their dedicated use of the King James Bible.

ACKNOWLEDGMENTS

I wish to express my deepest appreciation to the following people:

Chuck and Aimee Salliby, for financing the first printing of this book.

Rev. Robert Salliby, for the many hours he has spent proofreading this material and his valuable grammatical suggestions.

Rev. Robert Kelley, for his careful proofreading, especially of the Scriptural content of the manuscript, and for his helpful assistance with the Greek language.

Maureen Salliby, for her many hours of research, grammar checking, and ready assistance in whichever area she was needed.

CONTENTS

Introduction

Verse Comparisons 3

(topical headings of verse comparisons)
Redemption 3
Christ's Eternal Existence 10
Christ's Deity 11
Deity Provable In Christ As Judge 16
Christ The Creator 18
Christ The Son Of God 18
Virgin Birth 22
Also Concerning Christ's Birth 23
Christ's Incarnation 24
Christ's Omnipresence 25
Worship Of Christ 25
Christ's Commission 26
Christ's Miracles 28
Christ The Comforter 30
Christ's Teachings And Words 32
Christ's Teaching On Eternal Punishment 43
Christ's Teaching On Prayer And Fasting 46
Steps To The Cross, Trial, Crucifixion, And Resurrection 49
Ascension And Glorification Of Christ 54
Christ's Priesthood 56
Christ's Lordship 57
Christ's Grace 59
Christ's Return 61
Christ's Eternal Existence (Future) 62
Title "Lord" 63
Title "Christ" 64
Title "Jesus" 65
Names And Titles Of Jesus Omitted In The NIV 66

Footnotes 70
Some Background On The Corrupted Manuscripts 75
Current Indifference 87
Conclusion 93

Appendix 97
Notes 100
Index Of Verse Comparison Scriptures 101

INTRODUCTION

We, today, are living at a time when the attacks upon Jesus Christ find no equal in history. He is forbidden entrance into our educational system, maligned, cursed, and blasphemed by Hollywood; and seemingly fair game for every sick mind to vent its wildest imagination upon. However, the Christian should be shocked and absolutely scandalized to learn that the most devastating and irreparable of all such attacks is found in his modern translation of the Bible. And, while all other attacks can be dispensed with by merely considering their source, this one is official. A successful attack upon Jesus in the Bible, from which all knowledge of Jesus finds its source, can be more devastating to the eternal hopes of men than one can possibly imagine.

Almost as shocking as what is found in these Bibles is how it all passes unnoticed. Most Christians are entirely unaware that the Deity of Jesus, His attributes, character, redemptive work, teachings, etc. have been seriously damaged in these modern translations. Though they study these versions carefully, they never seem to notice what is missing or altered in them. Consequently, due to this ignorance, in no other area in which Christians are involved are their souls more vulnerable to the enemy.

To help counter the problem, this book was prayerfully prepared. A careful examination of its material will at least remove the ignorance.

Though all modern translations are guilty of corrupting the doctrine of Christ, one of the chief offenders is the New International Version (NIV). And yet, it is the most highly esteemed of the modern versions. In this book, we will compare its writings about Jesus with those of the crowned leader of all translations, the King James Version (KJV).

Please pray before turning this page. In Satan's warfare with the Church, on no other front is he accomplishing more than in the field of Bible corruption—which is due primarily to the blindness and indifference of the Church today. If he can keep you blind also, to his achievements here, he will. Pray: "God, give me Your discernment over all that follows. If You have something for me in this literature, then open my eyes and enable me to receive it graciously. Allow me to have nothing at all to do with anything that displeases You."

If you are about to conclude your reading here, having decided already that the forgoing claims are absurd and impossible to substantiate; be mindful of the wise counsel of Solomon, "He that answereth a matter before he heareth it, it is folly and shame unto him" (Prov. 18:13).

~ ~ ~ ~ ~ ~ ~ ~ ~ ~ ~ ~

Please note: In all of the following verse comparisons (1) All the words in the KJV that were omitted in the NIV are in **bold type.** (2) All the words in the KJV that were changed in the NIV are in [brackets] and underlined. (3) Three periods (...) before or four periods (....) after a verse of Scripture, means the verse did not begin or end there in the Bible.

If you do not use the New International Version but some other modern translation, please compare your Bible to the King James Version in the following verse comparisons. You will make some very surprising and needful discoveries.

VERSE COMPARISONS

REDEMPTION

Let us begin with redemption, the costliest plan of the ages. By the life-giving power of Christ's blood alone were we snatched from that landslide of humanity plunging to Hell and made to sit in Heavenly places. If we could fully comprehend, this side of eternity, the infinite difference between Heaven and Hell, we would fall on our faces and thank God after reading every reference to redemption in Scripture. Observe then, with tears, the omissions in the following verses.

(1) (Luke 9:56)

(KJV) **"For the Son of man is not come to destroy men's lives, but to save them.** *And they went to another village."*

(NIV) *"and they went to another village."*

(2) (Matt. 18:11)

(KJV) **"For the Son of man is come to save that which was lost."**

(NIV) (whole verse omitted)

It is shocking to see a whole verse of Scripture removed from the Bible, especially one as important as this one. Yet, they need only delete a word or two to destroy an entire truth, as we can see in the next verse comparison (3).

(3) (Matt. 9:13)

(KJV) *"...I am not come to call the righteous, but sinners* **to repentance**.*"*

(NIV) *"...I have not come to call the righteous, but sinners."*

If you were lost and wanted to become saved, which of these two lines would benefit you the most? What are the Scriptures saying here without the words "to repentance"? This incredible omission is deliberately repeated in Mark 2:17. While the words can be found in Luke 5:32 of the NIV, they appear wherever they belong in the KJV. By interpreting Luke correctly, the authors of the NIV should have acknowledged their mistakes in Matthew and Mark and not held back this valuable teaching that God wanted to appear three times in the Gospels.

READER'S NOTE: All acknowledge that the authors of the NIV were not personally responsible for all of the omissions and alternative readings found in their translation. Most of these are found in the texts that they translated from. However, the Traditional Text, held sacred by the Church throughout its history, was as available to them as it was to the authors of the KJV. And yet, in spite of this, they chose to employ inferior texts instead. Thus, they must be held responsible. If one tells a lie, is another less guilty who repeats it? Therefore, this writer feels justified in holding them personally accountable for whatever portions of Scripture have been altered in their version, and will treat each infraction as if they were its author. As in the case of my comments concerning their omission here in Matt. 9:13, all criticisms and accusations will be directed at them and not at the authors of their source documents.

(4) (Acts 8:37)

The only verse in the New Testament that shows both the minister in the act of sharing the Gospel and the listener receiving the gift of salvation is Acts 8:37. This verse also contains the only recorded account in Scripture (after the cross) of a sinner's actual confession of faith in Christ.

In answer to the Ethiopian eunuch's question, "what doth hinder me to be baptized?" we read:

(KJV) **"And Philip said, If thou believest with all thine heart, thou mayest. And he answered and said, I believe that Jesus Christ is the Son of God."**

(NIV) (whole verse omitted)

Incredible! Every reader of the NIV is eternally denied these precious lines.

---

(5) (Acts 9:5, 6)

Observe how the splendid dialogue between Jesus and Paul on the Damascus road is hacked up and condensed in the NIV. Keep in mind that this was Paul's very first believing experience.

(KJV) *"...***the Lord** *said, I am Jesus whom thou persecutest:* **it is hard for thee to kick against the pricks. And he trembling and astonished said, Lord, what wilt thou have me to do? And the Lord said unto him,** *Arise, and go into the city...."*

(NIV) *"...I am Jesus, whom you are persecuting, he replied. Now get up and go into the city...."*

---

(6) (Col. 1:14)

To create man, God merely "formed (him) of the dust of the ground, and breathed into his nostrils the breath of life." However, to re-create him, God had to first purchase him back with His own shed blood. Therefore, Col. 1:14 states:

(KJV) *"In whom we have redemption* **through his blood**, *even the forgiveness of sins:"*

(NIV) *"in whom we have redemption, the forgiveness of sins."*

Whether they were scrapping whole verses of Scripture or indispensable words like "through his blood," the translators of the NIV appear to have had no qualms at all.

Notice how Jesus is left out of His own redemptive work in the following six verse comparisons.

---

(7) (Gal. 6:15)

(KJV) **"For in Christ Jesus** *neither circumcision availeth any thing, nor uncircumcision, but a new creature."*

(NIV) *"Neither circumcision nor uncircumcision means anything; what counts is a new creation."*

---

(8) (Gal. 4:7)

(KJV) *"...thou art no more a servant, but a son; and if a son, then an heir of God* **through Christ**.*"*

(NIV) *"...you are no longer a slave, but a son; and since you are a son, God has made you also an heir."*

Just two words were left out, "through Christ." But where would redemption be without them?

---

(9) (Gal. 3:17)

(KJV) *"...the covenant, that was confirmed before of God* **in Christ**....*"*

(NIV) *"...the covenant previously established by God...."*

(10) (1 Cor. 9:18)

Paul said that he would—

(KJV) *"...make [the gospel]* **of Christ** *without charge...."*

(NIV) *"...offer [it] free of charge...."*

Compare also Rom. 10:15; 15:29.

---

(11) (Rom. 1:16)

(KJV) *"For I am not ashamed of the gospel* **of Christ**.*..."*

(NIV) *"I am not ashamed of the gospel...."*

---

(12) (John 6:47)

Jesus Himself said:

(KJV) *"Verily, verily, I say unto you, He that believeth* **on me** *hath everlasting life."*

(NIV) *"I tell you the truth, he who believes has everlasting life."*

Clearly, the key words in this text are "on me." In fact, without those words the verse tells us virtually nothing. It is vague and wide open to misinterpretation. Why then are they missing in the NIV, when not only this text but also our entire religion is built upon them? Their removal not only closed the door to Jesus alone being the object of all faith, but also opened the door to many other possibilities. Might not a non-Christian, for example, point sinners to some other means of salvation and use Jesus' words here to do it? If we indeed fear God, such tampering with Scripture should cause us to tremble.

Observe how we are left out of the redemptive plan in the next two verse comparisons.

---

(13) (1 Pet. 4:1)

(KJV) *"Forasmuch then as Christ hath suffered **for us** in the flesh...."*

(NIV) *"Therefore, since Christ suffered in his body...."*

---

(14) (1 Cor. 5:7)

(KJV) *"...Christ our passover is sacrificed **for us**:"*

(NIV) *"...Christ, our Passover lamb, has been sacrificed."*

Of all the words in this verse that they might have carelessly omitted, why those two words, "for us"? The answer is simple; none of this was carelessness. It was all a deliberate attempt to impair God's Word and, as a result, its readers.

---

(15) (1 John 5:13)

John gave us these reasons for writing his epistle, "that ye may know that ye have eternal life—

(KJV) **...and that ye may believe on the name of the Son of God.**"

(NIV) (omitted)

---

(16) (Eph. 4:6)

Look at the single word that was removed in this verse.

Notice too, how its absence lends credibility to the heresy that advocates that all men are saved regardless of their relationship with Jesus.

Paul, when writing to the Christians at Ephesus, explained that there is—

(KJV) *"One God and Father of all, who is above all, and through all, and in* **you** *all."*

(NIV) *"one God and Father of all, who is over all and through all and in all."*

Since an entire doctrine can be structured on the foundation of a single word, the removal of that word can, as well, cause the entire doctrine to collapse. The removal of the word "you," that has the purpose here of specifying that only the saints are being addressed, does as much damage to the truth as it would to remove the word "again" from "Ye must be born again" in John 3:7.

How easily an unsaved person, aware of Eph. 4:6 in the NIV, could embarrass the Christian witness by showing him in his NIV that salvation through Jesus is not necessary at all—since everyone has fellowship with God already. Should we wonder then why even advocates of the NIV have cautioned others not to use it when witnessing?

---

(17) (Rev. 21:24)

As it concerned New Jerusalem, John taught:

(KJV) *"And the nations* **of them which are saved** *shall walk in the light of it...."*

(NIV) *"The nations will walk by its light...."*

---

(18) (Acts 28:29)

After Paul's last recorded words in the Book of Acts (when he had preached salvation through Christ to the Jews) both he and his message, it would seem, were rejected. We see this, here in Acts 28:29.

(KJV) **"And when he had said these words, the Jews departed, and had great reasoning among themselves."**

(NIV) (whole verse omitted)

The translators of the NIV might have felt somewhat at home in that group.

CHRIST'S ETERNAL EXISTENCE

Leaving the subject of Jesus Christ's redemptive work, let us begin now to look at Jesus Himself—His Person, attributes, teachings, works, etc. We will begin with His eternal pre-existence and Deity and then, after considering His life here on earth, consider His eternal existence yet to come.

(19) (Mic. 5:2)

For Jesus to be Divine, He had to be eternally pre-existent. And for us to know He always existed, we must find proof of this in Scripture. We find this proof in Mic. 5:2. In fact, as one well observed, there is not a verse of Scripture that dates God the Father any further back into eternity than this verse dates God the Son.

(KJV) *"But thou, Bethlehem Ephratah, though thou be little among the thousands of Judah, yet out of thee shall he come forth unto me that is to be ruler in Israel; whose goings forth have been from of old, [from everlasting]."*

(NIV) *"But you, Bethlehem Ephrathah, though you are small among the clans of Judah, out of you will come for me one who will be ruler over Israel, whose origins are from of old, [from ancient times]."*

The words "from everlasting" in the KJV make Christ eternally existent (without a beginning) while the words "from ancient times" in the NIV merely make Him very old—One Whose origin we are left to speculate on. Is it any wonder then why some finally conclude, as do the Jehovah's Witnesses, that Christ was created?

While it is painful to evidence such recasting of the truth, please consider carefully these facts: Though the authors of the NIV translated the Hebrew word [olam] "ancient times" in Mic. 5:2, they translated the same Hebrew word "everlasting" when it was used to describe God's love (Ps. 103:17), God's praise (Ps. 106:48), God's righteousness (Ps. 119:142), God's kingdom (Ps. 145:13), God's salvation (Isa. 45:17), God's kindness (Isa. 54:8), God's covenant (Isa. 55:3), God's light (Isa. 60:19), God's renown (Isa. 63:12), etc.—why not then God's Son in Mic. 5:2?

They also translated [olam] "everlasting" when describing such things as joy, disgrace, shame, contempt, a possession, a sign, a name of God's people, etc. Strangely, though, when the word was used to describe the name of our "Redeemer" in Isa. 63:16, they translated it this way: "Redeemer from of old is your name." The KJV reads: "redeemer; thy name is from everlasting." Such inconsistency had to be either careless or incompetent—and if neither, then deliberately criminal.

CHRIST'S DEITY

Although Protestantism is embroiled in numerous doctrinal debates, one thing that all Christians must believe and be unanimously agreed upon is the Deity of Jesus Christ—that He is God. If we believe that He was merely a prophet or some other personage other than God, we have a "make believe" Jesus and, as a result of such faith, a "make believe" salvation. In light of this, please examine the following verse comparisons carefully.

(20)   (1 Tim. 3:16)

1 Tim. 3:16 has always been for the Church universal one of its strongest proof texts of Jesus' Deity.

(KJV) *"And without controversy great is the mystery of godliness: [God] was manifest in the flesh, justified in the Spirit, seen of angels, preached unto the Gentiles, believed on in the world, received up into glory."*

(Notice, how by changing one word in the passage, the NIV overthrows its highest meaning.)

(NIV) *"Beyond all question, the mystery of godliness is great: [He] appeared in a body, was vindicated by the Spirit, was seen by angels, was preached among the nations, was believed on in the world, was taken up in glory."*

Jesus is "God" in the KJV, but who "He" is in the NIV is ambiguous. The translators of the NIV made an attempt at fair play by admitting in a footnote that some manuscripts have the word "God." This, however, is as misleading as their text. The vast majority of ancient manuscripts support the reading of the KJV while only a handful support the reading in the NIV.

Besides, their rendering of 1 Tim. 3:16 is entirely wanting. How Paul, who so carefully identified in this passage: the mystery of godliness, the flesh, the Spirit, angels, Gentiles, the world, (and) glory, would have not supplied us with the identity of the One to Whom these all pertain, but just left us with a vague "he," is remarkable. The word "God" was not unknown to Paul who, in fact, used it twenty-two times in 1 Timothy.

Interesting too, as if the rewording of 1 Tim. 3:16 was expected, the very next two verses forewarn: "Now the Spirit speaketh expressly, that in the latter times some shall depart from the faith, giving heed to seducing spirits, and doctrines of devils; Speaking lies in hypocrisy; having their conscience seared with a hot iron."

---

(21) (Phil. 2:5, 6)

To be Divine, Jesus must also be equal to His Father. Phil. 2:5, 6 definitely states that He is.

(KJV) *"...Christ Jesus: Who, being in the form of God, [thought it not robbery to be equal with God]:"*

(Compare this carefully with the same text in the NIV.)

(NIV) *"...Christ Jesus: Who, being in very nature God, [did not consider equality with God something to be grasped],"*

Not only does the NIV misinform the reader in this passage but it also clearly argues against all of the facts. That Jesus believed He was God and equal to His Father, can be evidenced in John 5:18, 23; 8:58; 10:30; 14:9; 20:28, 29; and in a number of other Scriptures.

---

(22) (Rev. 1:8-13)

(KJV) *"I am Alpha and Omega, **the beginning and the ending**, saith the Lord, which is, and which was, and which is to come, the Almighty."* (9) *"I John, who also am your brother, and companion in tribulation, and in the kingdom and patience of Jesus **Christ**, was in the isle that is called Patmos, for the word of God, and for the testimony of Jesus **Christ**."* (10) *"I...heard behind me a great voice, as of a trumpet,"* (11) *"Saying, **I am Alpha and Omega, the first and the last:** and, What thou seest, write in a book...."* (12) *"And I turned to see...And being turned, I saw seven golden candlesticks;"* (13) *"And in the midst of the seven candlesticks one like unto [the Son of man]...."*

(These six verses abound with titles and eternal characteristics of Christ and leave no doubt in the reader's mind that Jesus is "the Almighty" of verse 8. At least as it reads in the KJV. However, this is not the case in the NIV.)

(NIV) *"I am the Alpha and the Omega, says the Lord God, who is, and who was, and who is to come, the Almighty."* (9) *"I, John, your brother and companion in the suffering and kingdom and patient endurance that are ours in Jesus, was on the island of Patmos because of the word of God and the testimony of Jesus."* (10) *"...I heard behind me a loud voice like a trumpet,"* (11) *"which said: Write on a scroll what you see...."* (12) *"I turned around to see...And when I turned I saw seven golden lampstands,"* (13) *"and among the lampstands was someone like [a son of man]...."*

Notice first that the NIV left out the following words that all pertain to Christ: "the beginning and the ending" in verse 8, "Christ" (twice) in verse 9 and, "I am Alpha and Omega, the first and the last" in verse 11. Then, the NIV changed "the Son of man" (as Jesus is called eighty-seven times in the New Testament) to "someone like a son of man" in verse 13. By these alterations not only is the reader of the NIV minus the marvelous revelation of Jesus found in the KJV; but also, since the NIV inserted the word "God" in after the word "Lord" in verse 8, the reader is bound to conclude that "the Almighty" refers here to God the Father.

---

(23)   (1 John 5:7, 8)

A verse Christians turn to with confidence, not only to substantiate Christ's Deity, but also because it provides the strongest Scriptural evidence of the Trinity, is 1 John 5:7. Notice carefully how this verse was thinned down in the NIV; and how, by blending what they left of it with verse 8, its most important teaching was swept off of the Bible page.

(KJV) *"For there are three that bear record* **in heaven, the Father, the Word, and the Holy Ghost: and these three are one."** (8) **"And there are three that bear witness in earth**, *the Spirit, and the water, and the blood: and these three agree in one."*

(NIV) *"For there are three that testify:"* (8) *"the Spirit, the water and the blood; and the three are in agreement."*

See Edward F. Hills, *The King James Version Defended*, pp. 209-213, for his defense of 1 John 5:7.

---

(24)   (1 Pet. 3:15)

(KJV) *"But sanctify the [Lord God] in your hearts...."*

(NIV) *"But in your hearts set apart [Christ as Lord]...."*

Since it is Christ Who dwells in our hearts by faith according to Eph. 3:17, one could easily assume that Christ is the One being referred to here in 1 Pet. 3:15. As we can see, even the scholars who reworded it thought so. However, while you can point to Christ's Deity in the stronger expression "Lord God" of the KJV, the NIV prevents this with its less convincing "Christ as Lord."

---

(25) (Jude 25)

Please study the differences here carefully.

(KJV) *"To the only **wise** God our Saviour, be glory and majesty, dominion and power, both now and ever. Amen."*

(Notice the additional words that were added in the NIV. These are underlined.)

(NIV) *"to the only God our Savior be glory, majesty, power and authority, <u>through Jesus Christ our Lord, before all ages</u>, now and forevermore! Amen."*

Out of twenty-three other references in the New Testament to the word "Saviour," fifteen of them definitely refer to Jesus, and possibly five or more of the remaining eight do as well. Furthermore, 1 John 4:14 acknowledges: "that the Father sent the Son to be the Saviour of the world." On the basis of these facts, one could make a very strong case for Jesus being the One that Jude referred to here, when he spoke of "God our Saviour," and afford us one more text in which Jesus is called God—at least as it stands in the KJV. However, by adding the words "through Jesus Christ our Lord," the NIV closed the door on that possibility altogether. The words "God our Saviour" in the NIV can only belong to God our Father.

Besides, what happened to the word "wise," "the only wise God"? The NIV removed the same word from an identical expression in 1 Tim. 1:17 where Paul also made mention of "the only wise God" (KJV). The NIV reads: "the only God."

(26) (Acts 15:18)

Acts 15:16, 17 reads: "After this I will return, and will build again the tabernacle of David, which is fallen down; and I will build again the ruins thereof, and I will set it up: That the residue of men might seek after the Lord, and all the Gentiles, upon whom my name is called, saith the Lord, who doeth all these things." That these verses apply to Jesus, there can be no doubt. The very next words in verse 18 continue the thought and, if they also apply to Jesus, offer more evidence of His Deity.

(KJV) *"Known* **unto God are all his works** *from the beginning of the world."*

(NIV) *"that have been known for ages."* (This is the entire verse.)

Not only is the intent seemingly apparent, but also the presentation is shoddy. When the verses were originally structured, were they allowed to say so little?

DEITY PROVABLE IN CHRIST AS JUDGE

(27) (Rom. 14:10-12)

Sometimes the attacks upon the Deity of Jesus are so subtle that they almost escape detection. Before considering an example of this, let us be reminded that John 5:22 tells us: "the Father judgeth no man, but hath committed all judgment unto the Son." Therefore, whenever the Scriptures speak of Divine "judgment," it should be understood that Christ is the Judge. Observe carefully then, in the following verses of the KJV, how "Christ" in verse 10 is, obviously, the One called "God" in verse 11 and the One called "God" again in verse 12.

(KJV) *"...for we shall all stand before the [judgment seat of Christ]."* (11) *"For it is written, As I live, saith the Lord, every knee shall bow to me, and every tongue shall confess to God."* (12) *"So then every one of us shall give account of himself to God."*

(So "God," Who we will give an account to in verses 11 and 12, is clearly "Christ" Who sits on the judgment seat in verse 10. Now see if the NIV offers the same evidence of Christ's Deity.)

(NIV) *"...For we will all stand before [God's judgment seat]."* (11) *"It is written: As surely as I live, says the Lord, every knee will bow before me; every tongue will confess to God."* (12) *"So then, each of us will give an account of himself to God."*

By replacing the words "judgment seat of Christ," as they are found in the KJV, with "God's judgment seat" in the NIV, they closed the door on this quiet yet valuable proof text of Christ's Deity.

---

(28) (Rev. 20:12)

We find a similar example in the "Judgment Day" scene of Rev. 20:12 where Jesus again is clearly the Judge.

(KJV) *"And I saw the dead, small and great, [stand before God]...."*

(NIV) *"And I saw the dead, great and small, [standing before the throne]...."*

The Deity of Jesus is at once discernible in the KJV's "stand before God" but not at all in the NIV's "standing before the throne."

---

(29) (Heb. 10:30)

(KJV) *"...Vengeance belongeth unto me, I will recompense,* **saith the Lord**...."

(NIV) *"...It is mine to avenge; I will repay...."*

(30) (Rev. 14:5)

(KJV) *"And in their mouth was found no guile: for they are without fault **before the throne of God**."*

(NIV) *"No lie was found in their mouths; they are blameless."*

It is not certain that this verse depicts the judgment seat of Christ. Nevertheless, so that no one can teach that it might and thereby suggest that we have one more reference to Christ as God, the NIV shuts down that possibility completely.

The attacks upon His Deity by no means end here. We will see in other verse comparisons that the attacks continue. Also, in the section entitled "Footnotes," (pages 70-74) we will see the attacks are not always found in the Scriptures themselves, but sometimes they are found in a footnote.

CHRIST THE CREATOR

(31) (Eph. 3:9)

(KJV) *"...which from the beginning of the world hath been hid in God, who created all things **by Jesus Christ**:"*

(NIV) *"...which for ages past was kept hidden in God, who created all things."*

As surely as the Bible "is a lamp unto (our) feet," just as surely, each of these deletions dim the light a little more.

CHRIST THE SON OF GOD

(32) (Eph. 3:14)

(KJV) *"For this cause I bow my knees unto the Father **of our***

Lord Jesus Christ,"

(NIV) *"For this reason I kneel before the Father,"*

---

(33) (John 9:35)

Jesus asked the man born blind—

(KJV) *"...Dost thou believe on the [Son of God]?"*

(NIV) *"...Do you believe in the [Son of Man]?"*

Since two verses later Jesus acknowledged that He is this "Son of God," this passage has always served as a valuable proof text of His Deity—but not so in the NIV.

---

(34) (Acts 3:13)

These words are found in a sermon preached by Peter.

(KJV) *"...the God of our fathers, hath glorified [his Son] Jesus...."*

(NIV) *"...the God of our fathers, has glorified [his servant] Jesus...."*

Jesus is called the "Son of God" 46 times in the New Testament. And in 80 additional places He is referred to as God's Son. Now, over against these 126 references to Jesus being the "Son" of God, He is called the "servant" of God only once (in Matt. 12:18) and only because Matthew, in that instance, was quoting Isa. 42:1.

Would it not have been better, in keeping with the theme and the intent of the New Testament, for the authors of the NIV to have called Jesus God's Son here in Acts 3:13 rather than His servant? As one minister, Rev. Robert Kelley so aptly stated: "If we are 'no more a servant, but a son' (Gal. 4:7), how much more is

Jesus, the eternal Son of God, a Son and not a servant."

---

(35) (Acts 3:26)

Further along in that same sermon, Peter again called attention to Jesus as the Son of God, by saying:

(KJV) *"...God, having raised up [his Son]* **Jesus**...."

(NIV) *"...God raised up [his servant]...."*

Here they adopt the poorer choice of words again. And they even hide His identity further by daring to strike out the word "Jesus" from the text as well.
Compare also Acts 4:27 and Acts 4:30.

---

(36) (Matt. 24:36)

In Matt. 24:36, we find Jesus referring to His Father in the personal possessive sense as—

(KJV) *"...[my] Father...."*

(NIV) *"...[the] Father."*

The NIV also substituted Christ's expression "my Father" with the words "the Father" in the following seven verses: John 6:65; 8:28, 38; 14:12, 28; 16:10; 20:17.
Compare also Luke 11:2.

---

(37) (John 1:27)

John the Baptist in proper humility declared:

(KJV) *"He it is, who coming after me* **is preferred before me**...."

(NIV) *"He is the one who comes after me...."*

Each little expression such as "is preferred before me," like so many pieces in a puzzle, was designed to make its own contribution to the completed picture of Christ on the Bible page—His Person, works, character, incomparableness, etc. Yet, they are systematically left out wherever possible in the NIV. This is indeed a strange practice. While a secular book generally exaggerates the depiction of its main character, the NIV depreciates that of its own.

---

(38) (John 6:69)

Listen to Peter's outstanding confession of faith in John 6:69.

(KJV) *"And we believe and are sure that [thou art that Christ, the Son] of* **the living** *God."*

(NIV) *"We believe and know that [you are the Holy One] of God."*

The difference between "thou art that Christ, the Son of the living God" and "you are the Holy One of God" is so vast that one can hardly make a comparison. While many people or objects are called "holy" in the Bible: Jerusalem, ground, a mount, the law, hands, a kiss, apostles, prophets, angels, etc., only One could ever be called "that Christ, the Son of the living God." As we examine these two translations side by side, what a difference we see between the KJV's presentation of Jesus and that of the NIV.

Perhaps the reader should pause to consider just how serious a matter all of this is. This incredible subversion of Scripture, though right there before our eyes, is the least acknowledged, yet gravest problem the Church faces today. "If the foundations be destroyed, what can the righteous do?" (Psalm 11:3). If the Bible is deprived of its truth, believers, churches, denominations, seminaries, ministries, creeds, etc. that lean on it for support must themselves be brought down.

VIRGIN BIRTH

(39) (Luke 2:33)

Though the Gospel writers called Mary Christ's "mother," they never called Joseph Christ's "father," except when quoting others who, in conversation, mistakenly called him that. While this can be evidenced in the KJV, that is not always the case in the NIV.

(KJV) *"And [Joseph] and his mother marvelled at those things which were spoken of him."*

(NIV) *"The [child's father] and mother marveled at what was said about him."*

Replacing the word "Joseph" with the word "father" in this verse, injures the doctrine of the virgin birth as much as it would injure the doctrine of creation if one were to replace the word "God" with the word "angels" in Gen. 1:1. Needless to say, such a rewording of Gen. 1:1 would be impossible to accept.—So is Luke 2:33 in the NIV.

(40) (Luke 2:43)

Luke again referred to—

(KJV) *"...[Joseph and his mother]...."*

(NIV) *"...[his parents]...."*

The word "parents" belongs in Luke 2:27, 41 but not in verse 43.

ALSO CONCERNING CHRIST'S BIRTH

(41) (Luke 1:28)

To acknowledge how privileged Mary had become, to bear within her womb God's Son, part of the angel's greeting to her was—

(KJV) *"...the Lord is with thee:* **blessed art thou among women**.*"*

(NIV) *"...The Lord is with you."*

Since her conception of Jesus is what made her "blessed," the absence of the above expression does not diminish from her but, as always, from Him.

(42) (Matt. 1:25)

Among the scores of pitiful omissions found in the NIV is the following:

(KJV) *"...she...brought forth* **her firstborn** *son...."*

(NIV) *"...she gave birth to a son...."*

That single word "firstborn" makes Matt. 12:46, 47; 13:55, 56; John 7:3-10; Gal. 1:19, and other Scriptures much easier to explain. Its absence makes the Catholic heresy of the perpetual virginity of Mary much easier to base Scripturally.

CHRIST'S INCARNATION

Observe the injuries done to the Incarnation (when God became man) in the following verse comparisons.

(43) (Eph. 5:30)

(KJV) *"For we are members of his body,* **of his flesh, and of his bones.***"*

(NIV) *"for we are members of his body."*

(44) (Acts 2:30)

Acts 2:30 speaks of the promise that God made to David.

(KJV) *"...that of the fruit of his loins,* **according to the flesh, he would raise up Christ** *to sit on his throne;"*

(NIV) *"...that he would place one of his descendants on his throne."*

(45) (1 John 4:3)

(KJV) *"And every spirit that confesseth not that Jesus* **Christ is come in the flesh** *is not of God...."*

(NIV) *"but every spirit that does not acknowledge Jesus is not from God...."*

CHRIST'S OMNIPRESENCE

(46) (John 3:13)

John 3:13 is a verse the Church has treasured for ages because it confirms that Christ's omnipresence (His Divine ability to be everywhere at once) was, surprisingly, never interrupted—not even while here during His life on earth.

(KJV) *"And no man hath ascended up to heaven, but he that came down from heaven, even the Son of man* **which is in heaven**.*"*

(NIV) *"No one has ever gone into heaven except the one who came from heaven—the Son of Man."*

Why were these vital words removed? Was it because they lent evidence to the Deity of Christ? Whatever the reason, it is a regrettable omission since we have nothing left in Scripture that reveals this unique and unexpected side of His omnipresence.

Dear reader, there can be no explanation why key lines like this one were targeted, apart from the obvious. It was a hellish scheme to deface and de-emphasize Jesus in Scripture. A conspiracy that began in the ancient world and that has come to the full in our modern translations of the Bible.

WORSHIP OF CHRIST

In the four Gospels, eleven accounts are found of people worshipping Jesus. The KJV faithfully gives us all eleven, while the NIV, only six. The NIV's wording of the other five accounts suggest something other than worship. Here are two examples.

(47) (Matt. 9:18)

(KJV) *"...behold, there came a certain ruler, and [worshipped him]...."*

(NIV) *"...a ruler came and [knelt before him]...."*

There is a vast difference between "worshipped" and "knelt before." One might kneel before a king but they do not worship him.

---

(48) (Matt. 8:2)

(KJV) *"And, behold, there came a leper and [worshipped him]...."*

(NIV) *"A man with leprosy came and [knelt before him]...."*

It would appear that the authors of the NIV had all kinds of difficulty translating the Greek word [proskuneo] "worship," nearly half of the time it was applied to Jesus. Yet, they had no difficulty at all translating the same word "worship" when it was used for worshipping a fellow servant (Rev. 19:10), an angel (Rev. 22:8), false religion (John 4:20, 22), idols (Acts 7:43), the image of the beast (Rev. 13:15; 16:2; 19:20), the beast (Rev. 13:4, 8, 12), the beast and the image (Rev. 14:9, 11; 20:4), demons and idols (Rev. 9:20), and even "the dragon" (Satan) (Rev. 13:4).

Frankly, it should be an embarrassment to the Church today to see so many Bible teachers continuously questioning various words in the King James Version and telling us how, in their opinion, they should have been translated, who are completely oblivious to such an obvious attempt as this one to bring down an entire doctrine.

Compare also Matt. 15:25; 20:20; Mark 5:6.

CHRIST'S COMMISSION

(49) (Acts 15:18)

As Acts 15:16, 17 make clear, the word "works" in Acts 15:18 largely applies to the life and work of Jesus.

(KJV) *"Known **unto God are all his works** from the beginning of the world."*

(NIV) *"that have been known for ages."*

This is the entire verse as it appears in the NIV.

---

(50) (John 9:4)

Jesus acknowledged His commission when He stated emphatically:

(KJV) "*[I] must work the works of him that sent me....*"

(NIV) "*...[we] must do the work of him who sent me....*"

---

(51) (Luke 2:49)

(KJV) "*...wist ye not that [I must be about my Father's business]?*"

(NIV) "*...Didn't you know [I had to be in my Father's house]?*"

---

(52) (Acts 7:37)

As it concerned Christ's commission, Stephen (while quoting Moses) stated:

(KJV) "*...A prophet shall* **the Lord your** *God raise up...***him shall ye hear**.*"*

(NIV) "*...God will send you a prophet....*"

Expressions like "him shall ye hear" the translators of the NIV neither wished to record nor, as we can see by their work, give heed to. May God help them.

CHRIST'S MIRACLES

Observe in this section how several of Christ's miracles, and the people's excitement over Him, are played down in the NIV.

---

(53) (John 5:4)

John furnished this important background for the miracle of healing that Jesus performed at the pool of Bethesda.

(KJV) **"For an angel went down at a certain season into the pool, and troubled the water: whosoever then first after the troubling of the water stepped in was made whole of whatsoever disease he had."**

(NIV) (whole verse omitted)

Compare also John 5:3.

---

(54) (Luke 8:43)

Regarding the woman with the issue of blood, Luke the physician tells us that she—

(KJV) "**...had spent all her living upon physicians**, *neither could be healed of any,*"

(NIV) *"...but no one could heal her."*

---

(55) (John 11:41)

While both versions acknowledge the death of Lazarus, who Jesus had come to raise, the KJV drives home the truth by giving us, as always, the entire Word of God.

(KJV) *"Then they took away the stone* **from the place where the**

dead was laid...."

(NIV) *"So they took away the stone...."*

---

(56) (Mark 1:31)

When Jesus healed Peter's mother-in-law—

(KJV) *"...**immediately** the fever left her...."*

(NIV) *"...The fever left her...."*

---

(57) (John 6:11)

When Jesus fed the multitude—

(KJV) *"...he distributed* **to the disciples, and the disciples** *to them that were set down...."*

(NIV) (He) *"...distributed to those who were seated...."*

---

(58) (Mark 6:51)

After Jesus walked on the sea and calmed the storm, His disciples—

(KJV) *"...were sore amazed* **in themselves beyond measure, and wondered.**"

(NIV) *"...were completely amazed,"*

(59) (Luke 9:7)

(KJV) *"...Herod...heard of [<u>all that was done by him</u>]...."*

(NIV) *"...Herod...heard about [<u>all that was going on</u>]...."*

(60) (Mark 6:33)

Concerning Christ's personal popularity with the people, Mark wrote:

(KJV) *"...and many [<u>knew him</u>]...**and came together unto him.**"*

(NIV) *"But many...[<u>recognized them</u>]...."*

(61) (Mark 3:15)

Mark informs us that Christ gave His disciples—

(KJV) *"...power **to heal sicknesses, and** to cast out devils:"*

(NIV) *"...authority to drive out demons."*

CHRIST THE COMFORTER

(62) (Luke 4:18)

(KJV) *"...he hath sent me **to heal the broken hearted**, to preach deliverance to the captives...."*

(NIV) *"...He has sent me to proclaim freedom for the prisoners...."*

(63) (Luke 8:48)

With great tenderness, Jesus said to the woman with the issue of blood—

(KJV) "...**be of good comfort**: *thy faith hath made thee whole....*"

(NIV) "...*your faith has healed you....*"

---

(64) (Luke 10:19)

The warmer and stronger affirmation of Jesus—

(KJV) "...*and nothing shall* **by any means** *hurt you.*"

(is substituted with—)

(NIV) "...*nothing will harm you.*"

---

(65) (Luke 2:14)

At the birth of Jesus, angels proclaimed:

(KJV) "...*peace,* [*good will toward men*]."

(NIV) "...*peace* [*to men on whom his favor rests*]."

Do these two Bibles bear the same witness? While the Scriptures are supposed to settle all matters of doctrine, if two Christians in a Bible study were to present Luke 2:14 from each of these Bibles, they would certainly have a difficult time reconciling the matter.

CHRIST'S TEACHINGS AND WORDS

In this section, we will look at just some of the damage done in the NIV to the teachings and words of Jesus.

(66) (Matt. 5:44)

(KJV) *"...Love your enemies,* **bless them that curse you, do good to them that hate you**, *and pray for them which* **despitefully use you, and** *persecute you;"*

(NIV) *"...Love your enemies and pray for those who persecute you,"*

Since Christ's command here to "Love your enemies" can be one of the most difficult to obey, can we afford to be without any of His counsel on the matter?

(67) (Mark 11:26)

Consider how important this teaching of Jesus is to our very salvation. Then see how unimportant it was to the translators of the NIV.

(KJV) **"But if ye do not forgive, neither will your Father which is in heaven forgive your trespasses."**

(NIV) (whole verse omitted)

Even when it appears in the Bible, this teaching is not given the attention it deserves by Christians. Why then would anyone want to remove it?
Compare also Jas. 5:16.

READER'S NOTE: As it concerned the Revised Version of 1881, which was the first of a long line of corrupted translations, Brooke Foss Westcott stated: "The value of the revision is most clearly seen when the student considers together a considerable group of passages, which bear upon some article of faith. The accumulation of small details then produces its full effect."[1] Which is all to say, if the truth can be altered enough times in Scripture, though no single instance might even be noticeable, an accumulation of these is most definitely going to have an effect. Therefore, I am convinced that while a single tarnished Scripture might not impact the reader's relationship with Jesus, the large numbers of them that have been scattered throughout the Bible have been skillfully designed to destroy it.

---

(68) (Matt. 20:16)

(KJV) *"So the last shall be first, and the first last:* **for many be called, but few chosen.**"

(NIV) *"So the last will be first, and the first will be last."*

While the words are missing here in the NIV, some point out that they can be found in Matt. 22:14. They can be found in both places in the KJV. This startling statement has provoked countless saints to fear God and become more mindful of living overcoming lives. Was it not worth repeating? God felt that it was!

---

(69) (Mark 6:11)

Regarding those cities that would reject His disciples and their message, Jesus exclaimed:

(KJV) "...**Verily I say unto you, It shall be more tolerable for Sodom and Gomorrha in the day of judgment, than for that city.**"

(NIV) (omitted)

Whether it was intended for this reason or not, the absence of these words takes away from the roll of Christ as Judge and, thus, thins down further proof of His Deity.

(70) (Matt. 23:14)

(KJV) **"Woe unto you, scribes and Pharisees, hypocrites! for ye devour widows' houses, and for a pretence make long prayer: therefore ye shall receive the greater damnation.**"

(NIV) (whole verse omitted)

Again, any attempt to silence the voice of Christ, our Judge, is to silence as well the evidence of His Deity.

---

(71) (Mark 10:24)

(KJV) *"...Jesus answereth again, and saith unto them, Children, how hard is it* **for them that trust in riches** *to enter into the kingdom of God!"*

(NIV) *"...Jesus said again, Children, how hard it is to enter the kingdom of God!"*

We are given an entirely different teaching, and a rather somber one, when the words "for them that trust in riches" are left out.

---

(72) (Luke 4:4)

(KJV) *"And Jesus answered him, saying, It is written, That man shall not live by bread alone,* **but by every word of God.**"

(NIV) *"Jesus answered, It is written: Man does not live on bread alone."*

This verse might be called the bad conscience of the NIV's translation committee and their version of it a "trade mark" of their dubious skills. Certainly, the deletion of "but by every word of God" is worthy of a group that tore out or changed so much of the same.

Interesting too is that Paul's admonition in Rom. 13:9: "Thou shalt not bear false witness," must have served to overload their conscience also, because they removed those words from the Bible as well.

In view of what has just been noted, consider the following omissions from the Bible. Any one of these omitted statements might have convicted the ancients who corrupted the Scriptures and produced the manuscripts from which modern Bibles are translated.

---

(73) (Luke 9:55)

Jesus told two of His disciples who mishandled Scripture—

(KJV) "**...Ye know not what manner of spirit ye are of.**"

(NIV) (omitted)

---

(74) (Mark 7:16)

Jesus admonished a crowd to give heed to His teaching with these words:

(KJV) "**If any man have ears to hear, let him hear.**"

(NIV) (whole verse omitted)

---

(75) (Luke 20:23)

Jesus told others who tried to "take hold of his words"—

(KJV) "...**Why tempt ye me**?"

(NIV) (omitted)

Aside from the words of Jesus, here are some other statements that were removed from the Bible that might have also convicted those who corrupted the Scriptures.

---

(76) (Acts 23:9)

(KJV) "...**let us not fight against God.**"

(NIV) (omitted)

---

(77) (John 8:9)

(KJV) *"...they which heard it,* **being convicted by their own conscience,** *went out...."*

(NIV) *"...those who heard began to go away...."*

---

(78) (1 Tim. 6:5)

Paul spoke of men who were "destitute of the truth"—and then warned:

(KJV) "...**from such withdraw thyself.**"

(NIV) (omitted)

(79) (Phil. 3:16)

All Christians are encouraged to "walk by the same—

(KJV) ...**rule, let us mind the same thing.**"

(NIV) (omitted)

---

(80) (Gal. 3:1)

(KJV) "...*who hath bewitched you,* **that ye should not obey the truth**...."

(NIV) "...*Who has bewitched you?....*"

---

(81) (Rom. 14:21)

You are warned to do nothing—

(KJV) "...*whereby thy brother stumbleth,* **or is offended, or is made weak.**"

(NIV) "...*that will cause your brother to fall.*"

---

(82) (Rom. 10:15)

Paul referred to—

(KJV) "...*them that* **preach the gospel of peace, and** *bring glad tidings* **of good things!**"

(NIV) *"...those who bring good news!"*

---

(83)   (2 Cor. 2:17)

(KJV) *"...we are not as many, which [corrupt the word of God]...."*

(NIV) *"Unlike so many, we do not [peddle the word of God for profit]...."*

Unfortunately, many scholars and publishers do both. They corrupt the Scriptures and, with all of their sales promotion, peddle them for profit.

---

(84)

Getting back to the teachings and words of Jesus; here are more of His statements that can be found in the KJV that were omitted in the NIV. (All bold-faced words were omitted.)

Matt. 15:6 *"And honour not his father **or his mother**...."*

Matt. 19:9 *"**...and whoso marrieth her which is put away doth commit adultery.**"*

Mark 9:49 *"**...and every sacrifice shall be salted with salt.**"*

Mark 10:21 *"...come, **take up the cross**, and follow me."*

Rev. 2:13 *"I know **thy works, and** where thou dwellest...."* Compare also Rev. 2:9.

Luke 4:8 *"...Jesus answered **and said unto him, Get thee behind me, Satan**...."*

Mark 7:8 *"...ye hold the tradition of men, **as the washing of pots and cups: and many other such like things ye do.**"*

Mark 8:26 *"...Neither go into the town, **nor tell it to any in the** town."

Matt. 20:7 "...**and whatsoever is right, that shall ye receive.**"

Matt. 15:8 *"This people* **draweth nigh unto me with their mouth**...."

Mark 13:14 "...*the abomination of desolation,* **spoken of by Daniel the prophet**...."

Matt. 24:7 "...*there shall be famines,* **and pestilences**, *and earthquakes....*"

Luke 11:11 *"If a son shall ask* **bread** *of any of you that is a father,* **will he give him a stone**?...."

Matt. 5:22 "...*whosoever is angry with his brother* **without a cause** *shall be in danger of the judgment....*"

Those additional words "without a cause," are more easily understood in light of Eph. 4:26. Also, they alone can explain God's permission to be angry in Eph. 4:26.

Aside now from the omissions, notice how the following statements of Jesus were reconstructed in the NIV and given an entirely different meaning.

---

(85) (Matt. 18:22)

(KJV) "...*I say not unto thee, Until seven times:* [*but, Until seventy times seven*]."

(NIV) "...*I tell you, not seven times,* [*but seventy-seven times*]."

Compare also Luke 10:1 where the "seventy" in the KJV who were sent out to minister are "seventy-two" in the NIV.

(86) (Matt. 6:27)

(KJV) "Which of you by taking thought can [*add one cubit unto his stature*]?"

(NIV) "Who of you by worrying can [*add a single hour to his life*]?"

This contradiction is repeated in Luke 12:25.

(87) (Luke 14:5)

(KJV) "...Which of you shall have [*an ass*] or an ox fallen into a pit...."

(NIV) "...If one of you has [*a son*] or an ox that falls into a well...."

Since the "ass" and "ox" are somewhat equal to each other, they are both useful to the illustration. If Jesus began with the word "son," though, the most eminent of the species, He would have had all He needed to make His strongest possible point. The additional word "ox," in this case, would not have furthered the illustration at all, but rather, distracted from it.

(88) (Matt. 11:19)

(KJV) "...wisdom is [*justified of her children*]."

(NIV) "...wisdom is [*proved right by her actions*]."

(89) (Matt. 19:17)

(KJV) "...Why [<u>callest thou me good</u>]?...."

(NIV) "Why [<u>do you ask me about what is good</u>]?...."

(90) (John 14:2)

(KJV) "In my Father's house are many [<u>mansions</u>]...."

(NIV) "In my Father's house are many [<u>rooms</u>]...."

(91) (Mark 14:24)

(KJV) "...This is my blood of the **new** testament...."

(NIV) "This is my blood of the covenant...."

Compare also Matt. 26:28.

(92) (Luke 6:48)

Christ's reason for why the house that could not be shaken stood firm, was—

(KJV) "...it was [<u>founded upon a rock</u>]."

(NIV) "...it was [<u>well built</u>]."

(93) (Luke 9:62)

Jesus said: "No man, having put his hand to the plough, and looking back—

(KJV) *...is fit for the kingdom of God."*

(NIV) *"...is fit for service in the kingdom of God."*

A new convert reading both the KJV and the NIV would certainly wonder why, what he was told was the absolute Word of God, has so many optional readings.

(94)

All of the previous illustrations befit a translation that also reworded the following:

(KJV) *an angel* (NIV) *an eagle* (Rev. 8:13)

(KJV) *the Spirit* (NIV) *the light* (Eph. 5:9)

(KJV) *his house* (NIV) *her house* (Col. 4:15)

(KJV) *the synagogues of Galilee* (NIV) *the synagogues of Judea* (Luke 4:44)

(KJV) *I (John) stood upon the sand of the sea* (NIV) *the dragon (Satan) stood on the shore of the sea* (Rev. 13:1)

(KJV) *good things to come* (NIV) *good things that are already here* (Heb. 9:11)

(KJV) *alms of such things as ye have* (NIV) *what is inside the dish* (Luke 11:41)

(KJV) *he might know your estate* (NIV) *you may know about our circumstances* (Col. 4:8)

(KJV) *do his commandments* (NIV) *wash their robes* (Rev. 22:14)

(KJV) *us unto our God kings and priests* (NIV) *them to be a kingdom and priests* (Rev. 5:10) Compare also Rev. 1:6.

Furthermore, in Heb. 9:4, the NIV has the golden altar of incense (which the priests had to have access to twice daily) behind the vale with the ark of the covenant, where only the High Priest could go once a year. Etc., etc.

When we also take into consideration the word changes and omissions found in other modern translations, do we wonder why Bibles clash in Bible studies to the embarrassment of both the teacher and students? One frustrated pastor had to discontinue a Bible study. Not because his people disagreed, but because he could not get their Bibles to agree. I have personally been told of two such instances.

CHRIST'S TEACHING ON ETERNAL PUNISHMENT

(95) (Mark 9:45)

In this age of reckless living, when men want more than ever to make little of what the Scriptures have to say about eternal punishment, the NIV will be of great assistance to them.

For example, Jesus spoke of casting sinners—

(KJV) "**...into the fire that never shall be quenched:**"

(NIV) (omitted)

(96) (Mark 9:44)

In that same conversation, Jesus gave this woeful description of the horrors of Hell:

(KJV) "**Where their worm dieth not, and the fire is not quenched.**"

(NIV) (whole verse omitted)

(97) (Mark 9:46)

To drive home to our conscience the painful words in Mark 9:44, Jesus repeated them again in verse 46.

(KJV) **"Where their worm dieth not, and the fire is not quenched."**

(NIV) (whole verse omitted)

In fact, this statement was repeated three times by our Lord, in three separate teachings, in verses 44, 46, and 48. To reduce its force, the NIV omitted it entirely in verses 44 and 46 and gave us His words once in verse 48.

(98) (John 3:15)

Jesus promised that those who believe in Him—

(KJV) **"...should not perish...."**

(NIV) (omitted)

(99) (Luke 10:15)

He promised that Capernaum—

(KJV) *"...shalt [be thrust down to hell]."*

(NIV) *"...will [go down to the depths]."*

Compare also Matt. 11:23.

(100) (Mark 3:29)

Jesus said: "he that shall blaspheme against the Holy Ghost"—

(KJV) "...is [*in danger of eternal damnation*]:"

(NIV) "...is [*guilty of an eternal sin*]."

While, as promised, Hell's fire cannot be quenched, all efforts have been made in the NIV to douse them on the Bible page. We see even more of this watering down of the doctrine in the epistles.

(101) (2 Pet. 2:17)

In 2 Pet. 2:17, the words—

(KJV) "...*to whom the midst of darkness is reserved* **for ever**."

(are shortened to—)

(NIV) "...*Blackest darkness is reserved for them.*"

---

(102) (1 Thess. 2:16)

Concerning God's "wrath" toward unbelievers, who had hindered the spread of the Gospel, Paul said, it—

(KJV) "...*is come upon them* [*to the uttermost*]."

(NIV) "...*has come upon them* [*at last*]."

(103) (Col. 3:6)

Paul specifically stated:

(KJV) *"...the wrath of God cometh **on the children of disobedience**:"*

(NIV) *"...the wrath of God is coming."*

Laws that can be broken without fear of consequence are not likely to be kept. Therefore, it was essential that the doctrine of Divine punishment be found in the Scriptures, right alongside God's commandments. Why then was it deliberately removed from the NIV in so many places?

(104) (2 Pet. 3:10)

Peter prophesied: "the earth...and the works that are therein—

(KJV) *...shall be [burned up]."*

(NIV) *"...will be [laid bare]."*

CHRIST'S TEACHING ON PRAYER AND FASTING

(105) (Mark 13:33)

(KJV) *"Take ye heed, watch **and pray**: for ye know not when the time is."*

(NIV) *"Be on guard! Be alert! You do not know when that time will come."*

What happened to prayer?

(106) (Mark 9:29)

(KJV) "...*This kind can come forth by nothing, but by prayer* **and fasting.**"

(NIV) "...*This kind can come out only by prayer.*"

What happened to fasting?

(107) (Matt. 17:21)

(KJV) **"Howbeit this kind goeth not out but by prayer and fasting."**

(NIV) (whole verse omitted)

What happened to prayer and fasting? In view of such total disregard for essential Scriptures, perhaps we should ask what is happening to our religion? We had to be a Church nearly void of discernment to have overlooked all of this for so long. However, once discovered, we would have to be highly criminal to permit its continuance.

Be assured that if one could search the corridors of pagan religions he could never uncover a foe or falsehood –irrespective of how ruthless or cunningly devised– that could bring down the soul more routinely, systematically, and surely than this sheer devastation of Scripture.

With regards to fasting, the only instruction to fast in the epistles is found in 1 Cor. 7:5. The NIV removed the thought of such a thing there as well.

(108) (Acts 10:30)

Not only does the NIV do away with instructions to fast but also testimonies concerning it. For example, in Acts 10:30, Cornelius testified: "Four days ago—

(KJV) **...I was fasting until this hour**...."

(NIV) (omitted)

In 2 Cor. 6:5, Paul spoke of his "fastings" (KJV), however, the NIV uses the word "hunger" instead. There is a vast difference between fasting by choice and going hungry because there is simply no food to eat.

In 2 Cor. 11:27, Paul again spoke of his voluntary "fastings" (KJV); the NIV rendered it, "gone without food" with no mention of whether food was available to him or not.

Consider the NIV's mutilation of the famed "Lord's Prayer" in the next two references.

---

(109) (Luke 11:2)

(KJV) "...**Our** *Father* **which art in heaven**, *Hallowed be thy name. Thy kingdom come.* **Thy will be done, as in heaven, so in earth.**"

(NIV) "...*Father, hallowed be your name, your kingdom come.*"

---

(110) (Matt. 6:13)

(KJV) "*And lead us not into temptation, but deliver us* [*from evil*]: **For thine is the kingdom, and the power, and the glory, for ever. Amen.**"

(NIV) "*And lead us not into temptation, but deliver us* [*from the evil one*]."

No organization on earth can survive whose founding documents are so unsettled. Thank God; Jesus is coming soon!

Compare also Col. 1:3.

STEPS TO THE CROSS, TRIAL, CRUCIFIXION, AND RESURRECTION

(111) (John 5:16)

John informs us that the Jews persecuted Jesus—

(KJV) "**...and sought to slay him....**"

(NIV) (omitted)

(112) (Luke 11:54)

Luke tells us that the Pharisees provoked Jesus to say many things—

(KJV) "**...that they might accuse him.**"

(NIV) (omitted)

(113) (Matt. 20:22)

Jesus asked James and John, "Are ye able to drink of the cup that I shall drink of—

(KJV) **...and to be baptized with the baptism that I am baptized with**?...."

(NIV) (omitted)

Similar words are omitted in verse 23.

| (114) | (John 13:23) |

The tender scene at the last supper where John is—

(KJV) *"...leaning [on Jesus' bosom]...."*

(is entirely recast in the NIV's—)

(NIV) *"...reclining [next to him]."*

| (115) | (1 Cor. 11:24) |

(KJV) *"...Take, eat: this is my body, which is **broken** for you...."*

(NIV) *"...This is my body, which is for you...."*

| (116) | (Luke 22:64) |

After Jesus' arrest—

(KJV) **"...they struck him on the face...."**

(NIV) (omitted)

| (117) | (Luke 22:68) |

Jesus said to the Sanhedrin—

(KJV) *"...ye will not answer* **me, nor let me go**."

(NIV) *"...you would not answer."*

(118) (Luke 23:15)

Pilate reminded the chief priests and rulers of how he had sent them to Herod, saying:

(KJV) *"...for [I sent you to him]...."*

(NIV) *"...for [he sent him back to us]...."*

---

(119) (Luke 23:17)

Concerning Pilate's attempt to release Jesus, Luke explains:

(KJV) **"(For of necessity he must release one unto them at the feast.)"**

(NIV) (whole verse omitted)

---

(120) (John 18:40)

Concerning Barabbas, John informs us that he—

(KJV) *"...[was a robber]."*

(NIV) *"...[had taken part in a rebellion]."*

---

(121) (Luke 23:23)

Regarding the people's demand for Christ's crucifixion, Luke wrote:

(KJV) *"...And the voices of them* **and of the chief priests** *prevailed."*

(NIV) *"...and their shouts prevailed."*

---

(122) (Matt. 27:24)

Pilate's own testimony concerning Jesus was—

(KJV) *"...I am innocent of the blood of this **just** person...."*

(NIV) *"...I am innocent of this man's blood...."*

How sad that an irreligious person like Pilate could discern what the authors of the NIV could not.

---

(123) (Mark 15:28)

It was a highlight in the writings of the Gospel authors when they could turn to the Old Testament and show through a fulfillment of prophecy that Christ was indeed their promised Messiah. This was especially true when the fulfilled prophecy concerned His atonement at Calvary. We see an important example of this here in Mark 15:28.

(KJV) **"And the scripture was fulfilled, which saith, And he was numbered with the transgressors."**

(NIV) (whole verse omitted)

---

(124) (Matt. 27:35)

Here is another Old Testament prophecy that was fulfilled at Calvary.

(KJV) *"And they crucified him, and parted his garments, casting lots:* **that it might be fulfilled which was spoken by the prophet, They parted my garments among them, and upon my vesture**

did they cast lots."

(NIV) *"When they had crucified him, they divided up his clothes by casting lots."*

It does not matter, relative to their absence here, that these words can be found where they belong in John 19:24 of the NIV. That does not answer the perplexing question of why they were removed in Matt. 27:35. If they are not extracting an entire thought out of the Bible, they have a strange habit (and one to be observed) of taking away something from where it belongs, if it can be found additionally somewhere else. Thus, they wound rather than honor Scriptural truths that God deliberately repeated.

---

(125) (Luke 23:38)

To explain why the sign on the cross was worded differently in each of the Gospels, Luke tells us it was written—

(KJV) "...**in letters of Greek, and Latin, and Hebrew**...."

(Evidently, each was not worded the same.)

(NIV) (omitted)

---

(126) (Acts 2:27)

As it concerned Christ's death, Peter said while quoting the Psalmist:

(KJV) *"...thou wilt not [leave my soul in hell]...."*

(NIV) *"...you will not [abandon me to the grave]...."*

(127) (Acts 2:31)

Four verses later, Peter confirmed in his own words:

(KJV) "...[*his soul*] was not [*left in hell*]...."

(NIV) "...[*he*] was not [*abandoned to the grave*]...."

(128) (Luke 24:1)

On the first day of the week, the women from Galilee went to the tomb of Jesus—

(KJV) "**...and certain others with them.**"

(NIV) (omitted)

(129) (Luke 24:42)

After Christ's resurrection, His disciples—

(KJV) "...*gave him a piece of a broiled fish,* **and of an honeycomb.**"

(NIV) "...*gave him a piece of broiled fish,*"

These numerous omissions and word changes deny the reader of the NIV either the entire account or a fully factual one.

ASCENSION AND GLORIFICATION OF CHRIST

(130) (John 16:16)

Jesus Himself said, concerning His ascension—

(KJV) *"A little while, and ye shall not see me: and again, a little while, and ye shall see me, **because I go to the Father**."*

(NIV) *"In a little while you will see me no more, and then after a little while you will see me."*

With each omission, we see more evidence of the bad character of this version.

---

(131) (John 17:5)

The evening before Jesus died, He prayed:

(KJV) *"...O Father, glorify thou me [with thine own self]...."*

(NIV) *"...Father, glorify me [in your presence]...."*

Clearly, these two readings stand worlds apart. We, ourselves, will one day be glorified "in" God's presence (John 17:22); but only Jesus could ever be glorified "with" God Himself (John 13:31, 32).

Is it not reasonable to suppose that this was one more attempt to weaken the doctrine of the Deity of Christ?

---

(132) (Matt. 25:31)

(KJV) *"...then shall he sit upon the throne [of his glory]:"*

(NIV) *"...he will sit on his throne [in heavenly glory]."*

Although the change here is hardly noticeable, like so many of the other subtle changes, it wipes an entire truth right off of the Bible page. Observe the verse again. In the NIV, the heavens are glorious while in the KJV, it is Christ Who is glorious.

(133) (1 Pet. 4:14)

Regarding the glorification of Jesus by the saints, Peter stated:

(KJV) "**...on their part he is evil spoken of, but on your part he is glorified.**"

(NIV) (omitted)

What line of Scripture could better describe the difference between these versions?
As it concerns the glorification of God the Father, compare 1 Pet. 5:11.

CHRIST'S PRIESTHOOD

(134) (Heb. 7:21)

(KJV) "...*Thou art a priest for ever* **after the order of Melchisedec:**"

(NIV) "...*You are a priest forever.*"

While the omitted words do appear elsewhere in the NIV, they were supposed to appear here as well. I repeat, when the NIV is not defusing a truth, it will labor to put less emphasis upon it.
For a point of interest, the words "after the order of Melchisedec" are recorded exactly seven times in the Bible and always in reference to Jesus. The number seven in Scripture is a very important number to God. It stands for perfection and completion, as does our Lord Jesus Christ. The NIV recorded the statement six times. The number six, since it comes short of the perfect number seven, is the number of man in Scripture.

CHRIST'S LORDSHIP

(135) (1 Cor. 10:28)

(KJV) "**...for the earth is the Lord's, and the fulness thereof:**"

(NIV) (omitted)

Compare also Acts 7:30 where "an angel of the Lord" in the KJV is simply called "an angel" in the NIV.

(136) (Matt. 23:8)

(KJV) *"But be not ye called Rabbi: for one is your Master,* **even Christ***; and all ye are brethren."*

(NIV) *"But you are not to be called Rabbi, for you have only one Master and you are all brothers."*

Dear reader, if we fail to acknowledge the seriousness of all this, the corrupters will have accomplished their purpose. We are not dealing here with just any book, or with just any subject. We are dealing with the Bible and with its main subject, the Lord Jesus Christ! And since all truth concerning Jesus is both learned from and confirmed by Scripture, the slightest omission from Scripture is too much and should be more than any true Christian can tolerate.

By omitting the words "even Christ," the reader is left to determine for himself just who this "Master" is. Someone might reply, "It should be obvious Who He is." No; it can only be obvious IF THE BIBLE SAYS SO!

(137) (Matt. 23:10)

In verse 10 of the conversation referred to in the previous verse comparison, the NIV detracts even further from the

Lordship of Jesus.

(KJV) *"Neither be ye called [masters]: for one is your [Master], even Christ."*

(NIV) *"Nor are you to be called [teacher], for you have one [Teacher], the Christ."*

---

(138) (Heb. 3:6)

The writer of Hebrews refers to Christ—

(KJV) *"...as a son over [his own house]...."*

(NIV) *"...as a son over [God's house]...."*

The word "God's" appears nowhere in the original. Here, as in so many other instances, the authors of the NIV have given their readers not what they found in the original but what they assumed was the meaning. We find another instance of this in the next verse comparison (139).

---

(139) (1 Tim. 6:14, 15)

(KJV) *"...the appearing of our Lord Jesus Christ:"* (15) *"Which in his times [he] shall show, [who] is the blessed and only Potentate, the King of kings, and Lord of lords;"*

(NIV) *"...the appearing of our Lord Jesus Christ,"* (15) *"which [God] will bring about in his own time—[God], the blessed and only Ruler, the King of kings and Lord of lords,"*

In view of the text that precedes and follows this passage, it is difficult to determine whether the Father or Son is being referred to here. While conjecture has been strong in either case, the title

"King of kings, and Lord of lords" (uniquely Christ's in the New Testament) makes Jesus, for some, the preferred choice. However, the authors of the NIV attempted to finalize the debate with their invention again of the word "God" (twice recorded in verse 15) that is found nowhere at all in the original. Thus, by this method of interpretative translation, the Divine Person in this passage can only be God the Father.

READER'S NOTE: Additional words, not found in the original Greek text, are sometimes added into an English Bible to add greater flow to the reading. These additional words, however, were not inspired, so to distinguish them from the rest, they are flagged in some special way. In the KJV, all such words are *italicized.*

On the other hand, the NIV is often such a free translation (or paraphrase) the use of a signaling system here would have been nearly impossible. With so many additional words to flag, not only would it have aroused suspicion had the authors done so, but also it would have exposed the words that were skillfully added to steer one's attention away from the truth, as in the case here of 1 Tim. 6:15. Therefore, since it would not have been practical to flag these words and far too conspicuous if they did, they elected to do almost nothing. They simply penned their words right next to God's, and then published them all, as if they were one and the same. Hence, when a person studies the NIV, though he is never conscious of it, what he is actually reading is a very skillful blend of God's Word and man's. For example, he is not informed here in 1 Tim. 6:15, that he is reading the author's interpretation right along with the Scriptures. Since the additional words were not flagged, he confidently assumes that each word in the verse was taken directly from the original text.

---

(140)

The NIV changed the more personal and intimate expression "our Lord," to the less personal "the Lord," in these seven verses: 2 Cor. 11:31; Gal. 1:3; Phil. 4:23; 2 Thess. 3:6; 2 Thess. 3:12; Philem. 25; and Rev. 22:21. Compare also Rev. 11:8.

CHRIST'S GRACE

(141) (Col. 1:2)

Paul said: "by the grace of God I am what I am"—and what

thankful Christian could ever claim otherwise? Although we deserve our place in a hopeless Hell, through Christ's grace alone, we need never come to that horrible end.

(KJV) *"...Grace be unto you, and peace, from God our Father* **and the Lord Jesus Christ.**"

(NIV) *"...Grace and peace to you from God our Father."*

---

(142) (1 Thess. 1:1)

(KJV) *"...Grace be unto you, and peace,* **from God our Father, and the Lord Jesus Christ.**"

(NIV) *"...Grace and peace to you."*

---

(143) (Rom. 16:24)

(KJV) **"The grace of our Lord Jesus Christ be with you all. Amen."**

(NIV) (whole verse omitted)

To extinguish so casually whole verses of Scripture and, of all verses, those that apply to Jesus and our eternal hope in Him, the authors of the NIV could have had no fear of God at all.

---

(144) (Rom. 11:6)

Rom. 11:6 illustrates how entirely opposite grace is to works. The second half of the verse (as it regards salvation) reads:

(KJV) "...**But if it be of works, then is it no more grace: otherwise work is no more work.**"

(NIV) (omitted)

CHRIST'S RETURN

(145) (Matt. 25:13)

The return of Jesus will be for the Church –in the presence of a watching world– irrefutable proof that all it ever believed and stood for was true. Therefore, every promise of His return in Scripture should serve to still the saints and provoke sinners to repent. In view of this, note the unpardonable and clearly senseless omission in the following.

The strong concluding line of the parable of the ten virgins reads:

(KJV) "*Watch therefore, for ye know neither the day nor the hour* **wherein the Son of man cometh.**"

(NIV) "*Therefore keep watch, because you do not know the day or the hour.*"

If such mutilation of Scripture be the fruit of today's labors for God, the Church should be just as alarmed over the return of Christ as the world.

(146) (Rev. 11:17)

While directing their worship to God the Father, the twenty-four elders exclaimed:

(KJV) "...*We give thee thanks, O Lord God Almighty, which art, and wast,* **and art to come....**"

(NIV) "...*We give thanks to you, Lord God Almighty, the One who is and who was....*"

CHRIST'S ETERNAL EXISTENCE (FUTURE)

We considered earlier, how the NIV destroyed the eternal pre-existence of Jesus in Mic. 5:2. Observe now the veil it throws over His eternal existence yet to come.

---

(147) (John 8:35)

These are Christ's own words concerning His eternal existence.

(KJV) "...[*the Son abideth*] ever."

(NIV) "...[*a son belongs to it*] forever."

These are two entirely different statements. The expression "the Son" in the KJV refers to Jesus. The very next verse acknowledges this in both translations. However, "a son" in the NIV has no relevance to Jesus at all. The NIV capitalizes the letter "S" in "Son" when referring to Jesus as the "Son" of God.

---

(148) (Rev. 1:8)

After His return to Heaven, Jesus declared:

(KJV) "*I am Alpha and Omega,* **the beginning and the ending**...."

(NIV) "*I am the Alpha and the Omega....*"

---

(149) (Rev. 1:11)

Jesus also proclaimed:

(KJV) "...**I am Alpha and Omega, the first and the last**...."

(NIV) (omitted)

Although this is difficult to believe it is nevertheless true: The NIV and the rest of the modern versions of the Bible, have done more "official" damage to the Person of the Lord Jesus Christ, than all of the labors of a history worth of infidels heaped together.

---

(150) (Rev. 5:14)

Whether the worship in Rev. 5:14 is being directed to God the Father or God the Son is not clear, nevertheless, the NIV's pitiful omission from the verse is.

(KJV) *"...And the* **four and twenty** *elders fell down and worshipped* **him that liveth for ever and ever.**"

(NIV) *"...and the elders fell down and worshiped."*

Given such tools to work with, we can see that current Christianity is indeed on a perilous course.

TITLE "LORD"

(151) (1 Cor. 15:47)

We saw back in verse comparison (29) that the NIV had left the word "Lord" out in Heb. 10:30. Quite often this title, when it is applied to Jesus, does not appear in this translation. In fact, though it might seem impossible, the NIV removed this title from Jesus thirty-one times in the New Testament! Here is just one example.

(KJV) *"The first man is of the earth, earthy: the second man* **is the Lord** *from heaven."*

(NIV) *"The first man was of the dust of the earth, the second man from heaven."*

TITLE "CHRIST"

The title "Christ," was removed forty-five times in the NIV. Here are just three examples.

(152) (2 John 9)

John explained that the genuine Christian is—

(KJV) *"...He that abideth in the doctrine* **of Christ**.*...*"

(NIV) *"...whoever continues in the teaching...."*

(153) (1 Tim. 2:7)

Paul assured Timothy—

(KJV) *"...I speak the truth* **in Christ**.*..."*

(NIV) *"...I am telling the truth...."*

(154) (Phil. 4:13)

Paul also said confidently:

(KJV) *"I can do all things through [Christ] which strengtheneth me."*

(NIV) *"I can do everything through [him] who gives me strength."*

Who is "him"?

TITLE "JESUS"

(155) (Matt. 16:20)

The name "Jesus" was removed forty-six times in the NIV. Here is one very sad example.

(KJV) *"Then charged he his disciples that they should tell no man that he was* **Jesus** *the Christ."*

(NIV) *"Then he warned his disciples not to tell anyone that he was the Christ."*

This is certainly a pitiful omission since this is the only place in the four Gospels where Christ called Himself "Jesus." * The name Jesus means "Jehovah is Salvation" Whom Christ in this verse acknowledged Himself to be. Therefore, once again, the designs against Him appear to be self evident.

What is also worth noting is that while Jesus is referred to by many different names numerous times in the New Testament, it is seldom that Jesus (except for the one title "Son of man") referred to Himself by any name. Yet, wherever He did, the NIV has removed these names from His own words in thirteen places. The Revised Version of 1881 only removed them ten times. If the trend continues, translations of the future might remove them wherever Jesus laid claim to His titles and cause some to believe that Jesus was not "Jesus," "the Christ," "Son of God," "Son of man," "Alpha and Omega," etc. because He never personally claimed to be. These, they might conclude, were simply inappropriate titles His misinformed followers gave to Him.

I repeat, it is a strange book that continually tears away at rather than builds up its main Character.

---

* Our Lord also used the title in John 17:3, but He did not call Himself "Jesus" in that verse as He did in Matt. 16:20.

It would have taken many more pages to record all of the verses where a title for Jesus that appears in the KJV was omitted in the NIV. For the reader's examination, though, the following list is provided.

NAMES AND TITLES OF JESUS OMITTED IN THE NIV

Matt. 8:29 .... Jesus	John 19:38 .... Jesus	Gal. 4:7 .... Christ
Matt. 9:28 .... Jesus	John 20:15 .... Jesus	Gal. 6:15 .... Christ Jesus
Matt. 13:36 .... Jesus	John 21:5 .... Jesus	Gal. 6:17 .... Lord
Matt. 13:51 .... Lord	John 21:21 .... Jesus	Eph. 3:9 .... Jesus Christ
Matt. 15:30 .... Jesus'	Acts 2:30 .... Christ	Eph. 3:14 Lord Jesus
Matt. 16:20 .... Jesus	Acts 3:13 ....*his Son	.... Christ
Matt. 17:20 .... Jesus	Acts 3:23 .... prophet	Phil. 4:13 .... Christ
Matt. 17:22 .... Jesus	Acts 3:26 ....*his Son	Col. 1:2 Lord Jesus
Matt. 18:2 .... Jesus	Acts 3:26 .... Jesus	.... Christ
Matt. 18:11 ..... Son of man	Acts 4:27 ....*holy child	Col. 1:28 .... Jesus
Matt. 19:16 ..*Good Master	Acts 4:30 ....*holy child	1 Thess. 1:1 Lord Jesus
Matt. 23:8 .... Christ	Acts 7:30 .... Lord	.... Christ
Matt. 23:10 ....*Master	Acts 8:37 .... Jesus Christ	1 Thess. 2:19 .... Christ
Matt. 24:2 .... Jesus	Acts 8:37 .... Son of God	1 Thess. 3:11 .... Christ
Matt. 25:13 ..... Son of man	Acts 9:5 .... Lord	1 Thess. 3:13 .... Christ
Matt. 27:24 ...... just person	Acts 9:6 .... Lord (twice)	2 Thess. 1:8 .... Christ
Matt. 28:6 .... Lord	Acts 9:29 .... Jesus	2 Thess. 1:12 .... Christ
Mark 2:19 .... bridegroom	Acts 15:11 .... Christ	1 Tim. 1:1 .... Lord
Mark 5:13 .... Jesus	Acts 15:18 .... God	1 Tim. 2:7 .... Christ
Mark 7:27 .... Jesus	Acts 16:31 .... Christ	1 Tim. 3:16 .... God
Mark 9:24 .... Lord	Acts 19:4 .... Christ	1 Tim. 5:21 .... Lord
Mark 11:10 .... Lord	Acts 19:10 .... Jesus	2 Tim. 4:1 .... Lord
Mark 11:14 .... Jesus	Acts 20:21 .... Christ	2 Tim. 4:22 .... Jesus Christ
Mark 14:18 .... Jesus	Acts 22:16 .... Lord	Titus 1:4 .... Lord
Mark 14:45 master (or	Rom. 1:16 .... Christ	Philem. 6 .... Jesus
.... Rabbi)	Rom. 6:11 .... Lord	Heb. 3:1 .... Christ
Luke 4:41 .... Christ	Rom. 14:6 .... Lord	Heb. 10:30 .... Lord
Luke 7:22 .... Jesus	Rom. 15:8 .... Jesus	1 Pet. 3:15 ....*God
Luke 7:31 .... Lord	Rom. 16:18 .... Jesus	1 Pet. 5:10 .... Jesus
Luke 9:35 ......*beloved Son	Rom. 16:20 .... Christ	1 Pet. 5:14 .... Jesus
Luke 9:56 .... Son of man	Rom. 16:24 Lord Jesus	1 John 1:7 .... Christ
Luke 9:57 .... Lord	.... Christ	1 John 4:3 .... Christ
Luke 13:25 .... Lord	1 Cor. 5:4 ..... Christ (twice)	1 John 5:7 .... the Word
Luke 17:6 .... Lord	1 Cor. 5:5 .... Jesus	1 John 5:13 ...... Son of God
Luke 22:31 .... Lord	1 Cor. 9:1 .... Christ	2 John 3 .... Lord
Luke 23:42 .... Lord	1 Cor. 9:18 .... Christ	2 John 9 .... Christ
John 4:16 .... Jesus	1 Cor. 10:28 .... Lord's	Rev. 1:8 the beginning
John 4:42 .... Christ	1 Cor. 15:23 .... Christ's	.... and the ending
John 4:46 .... Jesus	1 Cor. 15:47 .... Lord	Rev. 1:9 .... Christ (twice)
John 6:69 .... Christ	1 Cor. 16:22 .. Jesus Christ	Rev. 1:11 Alpha and
John 6:69 *Son of the	1 Cor. 16:23 .... Christ	.... Omega
.... living God	2 Cor. 4:6 .... Jesus	Rev. 1:11 the first and
John 8:20 .... Jesus	2 Cor. 4:10 .... Lord	.... the last
John 8:35 .... the Son	2 Cor. 4:11 .... Jesus	Rev. 1:13 ....*Son of man
John 9:35 ....*Son of God	2 Cor. 5:18 .... Jesus	Rev. 12:17 .... Christ
John 11:14 .... Jesus	2 Cor. 10:7 .... Christ's	Rev. 14:14 ....*Son of man
John 11:39 .... Jesus	2 Cor. 11:31 .... Christ	Rev. 20:12 .... God
John 13:23 .... Jesus	Gal. 3:17 .... Christ	Rev. 22:21 .... Christ

An asterisk (*) indicates that the NIV substituted the title with an inferior one.

The forgoing is a rather impressive list of Jesus' names and titles that God inspired the ancient authors of Scripture to give us that modern translators felt we could do without.

In fairness, however, it should also be mentioned that there are at least 378 additional references to Jesus (by title) in the NIV that cannot be found in the KJV. These are as follows: The name "Jesus" occurs an additional 341 times, "Christ" an additional 17 times, "Lord" an additional 9 times, and all others an additional 11 times.

With regard to the same, however, the following should also be mentioned:

(1) Of these 378 additional titles, NOT ONE OF THEM can be found in the Traditional Text* from which the KJV was translated. A text, incidentally, that agrees with about ninety per cent of the ancient manuscripts that have been passed down to this present time.

(2) Only a few of these additional titles (roughly one out of every twenty) can even be found in the corrupted texts from which the NIV was translated. Even the oldest of the modern English versions, the Revised Version of 1881, that can generally be found in agreement with the NIV, only recorded 19 of these 378 additional titles. So, we can see that the vast majority of them were plainly invented by the NIV's translation committee.

(3) Although it is proper to italicize any additional words not found in the original text, none of these 378 extra titles were italicized, or flagged in any other manner, to show that they did not appear in the source documents.

(4) Lastly, the vast majority of these extra titles serve no purpose. For the most part, each one either replaced a pronoun that just as clearly referred to Jesus, or was plugged into a text that did not need the support of the additional title to inform the reader that it was dealing with Jesus.

All of the above should cause one to question why, in view of this overrun of nonessential unauthorized titles, were so many authorized titles of Jesus removed from the NIV, where it was necessary for the reader to have them. God knew where He wanted the name of Jesus in the Bible, as He did every other word, jot, or tittle. Therefore, whether His choices agree with our current ideas or not, or can be defended on grounds for which we find any sufficient reasoning at all, it is the duty of all translators of GOD'S WORD to provide for the reader GOD'S WORD. Or else they should entitle their book by some other name.

---

*The Traditional Text is the text that had been widely accepted and used by the Church throughout its history. It can be found in its entirety in what is commonly called the "Textus Receptus." ("Textus" Text, "Receptus" Received)

Obviously, the Church had better spend less time hunting New Agers and putting on concerts and more time paying attention to what is happening to its Bible.

Fellow Christian, there can be no justification for such senseless mishandling of the doctrine of Christ, nor can a defense be proposed that is adequate enough to absolve the Church for its approval of the same. Remember, to prevent such mistakes from occurring, God gives His people the Spirit of truth that they might discern the spirit of error. Therefore, these very translations we tolerate testify to how low we have sunk spiritually. If Jesus were here in person, would He champion these books as we do or order their destruction? The unhappy hour of "Laodicea" is certainly upon us.

However, all of this defacing of God's Word, with what was certain to follow—the deception of God's people, did not come without warning. Read carefully this prophecy: "But there were false prophets also among the people, even as there shall be false teachers among you, who privily shall bring in damnable heresies, even denying the Lord that bought them, and bring upon themselves swift destruction. And many shall follow their pernicious ways; by reason of whom the way of truth shall be evil spoken of. And through covetousness shall they with feigned words make merchandise of you: whose judgment now of a long time lingereth not, and their damnation slumbereth not" (2 Pet. 2:1-3).

Is it possible to overreact to this devastation of God's Word? By whose authority did any man qualify to presume upon the Scriptures this way—twisting, tarnishing, and scrapping Divine language? We would not take these liberties with other documents of the church, why then do we take these liberties with the Bible?

What is most appalling, however, is the current indifference to it all—ESPECIALLY AMONG PASTORS. It is remarkable how ministers will gather at councils and labor for days over the tiniest deletion or addition to their constitution or bylaws. Yet, it matters little to them that cardinal truths, upon which eternal souls depend, are hacked up and molested in the very Word of God. If ever men were guilty of straining at gnats and swallowing camels, surely these are today.

Dear Pastor, where do you stand on this issue? Unless you can propose a case (thus far unheard) that can warrant the injuries done to the Deity, Character, Teachings, Atoning work, etc. of Jesus Christ in modern Bibles, why do you minister to God's people from them?

Like the watchmen we are supposed to be, let us perceive behind which approaching shield lurks the real threat to the Church. It is not the IRS, secular humanism, the New Age Movement, or any other adversary real or imagined. Though a violent world, reinforced by every demon that exists, be committed to the destruction of the Church, if we through neglect are becoming deprived of the entire Bible, the greatest danger lies not outside our walls but within them.

~ ~ ~ ~ ~ ~ ~ ~ ~ ~ ~ ~

Dear Christian, where do you stand on this matter? Your opinion counts more, perhaps, than you care to believe. When Jesus declared to His Father in prayer, "I have given unto them the words which thou gavest me; and they have received them" (John 17:8), He acknowledged one of the greatest transferals of responsibility that had ever occurred. God the Father had given His words to God the Son, Who in turn had faithfully passed them on to us. (See also John 12:49, 50; 14:25, 26.) Consequently, every believer, from the minister to the most recent convert in the pew, is as responsible for the safe keeping of the New Testament as were its original authors and will be as accountable as they before the Judgment Seat of Christ for their part in its defense.

It should be engraved upon our conscience that the Bible, as well as the entire Christian religion, is presently in our hands and will be passed on to the next generation in whatever condition we leave it.

~ ~ ~ ~ ~ ~ ~ ~ ~ ~ ~ ~

So that what was just stated is not confused with what will be stated later on, let us pause to consider these facts: While men will corrupt the Scriptures, simultaneously, God will preserve them. In other words, though men will produce a score of defective Bibles, God will preserve a specimen of His genuine Word that He will hold apart from and above all others. This He promised in Ps. 12:6, 7; Isa. 40:8, and elsewhere.

So, there is a fine line to be drawn here. While we too are entrusted with the safe keeping of God's Word, we are to accomplish our part by simply leaving it alone. Though we all have the right to read, memorize, and employ its words, no one has the right to omit, add to, or change them. Hence, our defense of the Bible must always be: If God wrote it, let none dare touch it!

FOOTNOTES

Aside from the text, let us glance down now at the footnotes beneath the text; since here is where some of the greatest damage to the student of Scripture is done. I am not referring here to the footnotes that explain the Scriptures, but to those that critique and question them.—At which work, the authors of the NIV were masters.

Let us consider the following from the stand point of a brand new convert. When he opens the Bible, perhaps for the first time in his life, he will likely turn to the Gospels to begin his reading. As he reads along (if in the NIV) little letters in the text direct his attention to footnotes at the bottom of the page. Some of these footnotes provide cross-references, others explanations of words, and still others alternative readings. As he studies these together with the Bible, he also finds, quite frequently, a very disturbing type of footnote. This one informs him that certain Scriptures he read (that could vary from a single word to a large group of verses) are either missing or seriously reworded in some manuscripts. For example, after he reads Matt. 12:47, the letter (c) is found at the end of the verse. After that letter, at the bottom of the page, this footnote appears: "Some manuscripts do not have verse 47." Concerning the words "the God of Jacob" in Acts 7:46, the footnote reads: "Some early manuscripts *the house of Jacob*"— which is, obviously, a substantial difference.

By the time the new convert finishes reading the four Gospels, he will have also read at least ninety of these types of footnotes.—All of which, as in the above two examples, have either contradicted or denied some Scriptural truth. So, before leaving the first section of the New Testament that he was told he could trust and read with unquestioning faith, he was informed about ninety times that what he read in the Bible might not have been God's Word at all! If at this point he wishes to read the entire New Testament, he will have to get his confidence past at least fifty-seven more of these footnotes, leaving him to wonder, "Just what did God say?" Show me a babe in the Lord with conviction enough to survive that kind of pressure put on his faith.

When we consider the hurdles one must clear when beginning to run the Christian race, why was such an insurmountable one as this one needlessly added? Not only must the new convert believe and obey God's Word, but also he must first figure out what it is. A feat, quite obvious to him by now, that even theologians cannot accomplish. One young woman confessed that these footnotes would make her cry. Despairingly, she would close her Bible, and then pray later for the courage to read it again. We do not need a doctorate in theology to conclude that, while only God could write the text, anyone at all can write in the margin—such as a scholar with a doctrinal bent etc. And, once he establishes himself there as the reader's guide; he, rather than the Bible, becomes the final authority. By using one manuscript to correct another and groundless theories to cast doubt on relevant texts, he manipulates the reader who, torn between the Scriptures and the marginal notes that critique the Scriptures, will gradually lose faith in the Word of God and put his faith in the scholar instead.

Still others, when they have had too many Scriptures overturned by marginal notes, lapse off into a state of indifference to it all. Needing assurance and finding none, they eventually dismiss the Bible as a rather unconvincing book. Instead of it being a clear assuring light in the midst of darkness, the Bible becomes, for them, just another confused item in a world of confusion.

While some sense at once the injury coming on, for others the process works quietly behind their suspicions. As their eyes glance down at these footnotes on page after page and their mind tallies up one shattered Scripture after another, subconsciously layer after layer of their faith peels away. In either case, their convictions fatigue and gradually break down. Sure faith has to have a sure object. When the object wavers, the faith does likewise.

Here are a few examples of these footnotes; they are all based (according to the NIV) on the authority of other manuscripts. So that the reader can observe exactly what words the footnote is referring to, all verses in the following will be quoted from the NIV.

In Mark 1:1, where Jesus is called "the Son of God," the footnote makes this title highly questionable. It states: "Some manuscripts do not have *the Son of God.*"

In John 10:29 Jesus said: "My Father, who has given them to me, is greater than all." The footnote's alternative reads: "What my Father has given me is greater than all." Since, in this passage, the Christians are the ones God gave to Jesus, the footnote would suggest that Christians are greater than all. Is such a fact stated elsewhere in Scripture or consistent with anything else Jesus taught?

Regarding Acts 20:28, "Be shepherds of the church of God, which he bought with his own blood," the footnote takes issue with the strong expression "of God" by informing the reader that it could have been worded "of the Lord" instead. It is ironical to see a translation, that so casually mishandled the names and titles of Jesus throughout the New Testament, making any issue at all over the word "Lord" for the word "God" here in one of the clearest proof texts of Christ's Deity in Scripture. I believe their reasons are so apparent that they need no explanation at all.

1 Cor. 16:24 reads: "My love to all of you in Christ Jesus. Amen." Ironically, after the authors of the NIV left the words "Jesus" and "Christ" out of verse 22 and the word "Christ" out in verse 23, a footnote informs the reader concerning verse 24 that some manuscripts do not have the word "Amen." May God be merciful.

Where Jesus said in John 7:8, "I am not yet going up to this Feast" (a feast that He later attends in verse 10) the footnote suggests that the word "yet" does not belong in the text—when, obviously, the absence of this word would have meant Christ lied. Remember, Christians want to trust their Bible. Therefore, even subversive commentary on so noble a page does not become easily suspect.

Luke 22:43, 44 carries the famed account of the angel strengthening Jesus at Gethsemane, of Christ's earnest prayers while there, and how His sweat was like great drops of blood. The footnote suggests that these verses do not belong in the Bible.

Christ's matchless prayer of love that He prayed from the cross in Luke 23:34: "Father, forgive them, for they do not know what they are doing," the footnote implies does not belong in the Bible either. Truly, the accusation found in Romans 1:22, 25 is applicable here, "Professing themselves to be wise, they became fools...Who changed the truth of God into a lie." See also the footnotes for Matt. 12:47; 16:2, 3; 21:44.

This is merely a glimpse at the spectacle that can be found there at the bottom of the page. Now, while all the footnotes recorded above were based on the authority of other manuscripts (as is stated in the NIV), there are still other footnotes that are merely presented as alternative readings. These also, on occasion, become very disturbing to the reader.

For example, Jesus said in John 10:9 "whoever enters through me will be saved." The footnote's alternative for "will be saved," is "kept safe" instead.

In Matt. 16:18 Jesus said: "you are Peter, and on this rock I will build my church." In view of the confusion caused by a misinterpretation of this verse that has held millions in heathen darkness down through the ages, one would suppose that if the authors of the NIV were going to make any comment on the verse at all, they would have given us the standard Protestant interpretation and helped clear up some of the confusion. Instead, they did the opposite. Their footnote reads: "*Peter* means *rock*," and after that, it has no more to say—leaving the novice to conclude that Peter is the rock that Christ will build His Church upon. Which, of course, all conforms well with the heresy long held by the Roman Catholic Church that Peter is this rock and also their first Pope. Therefore, they believe that Rome holds the exclusive rights to the religion of Jesus Christ.

Aside from our interest here in the footnote, it is also worth mentioning that in spite of the size and strength of the Roman Catholic Church and its dominance among the world's religions, it is actually quite fragile. Its entire structure and dogma hangs on a fine thread –its interpretation of this verse– and if it can be disproved here, the thread would break, and the colossus would collapse. The word "Peter" is [petros] in Greek and means a piece of rock. The word "rock" that Jesus promised to build His Church upon is [petra] in Greek and means a mass of rock. These two "rocks" could be as opposite as a pebble is to the rock of Gibraltar. "Who is a rock, save our God?" (2 Sam. 22:32).

For the wording in Rom. 9:5: "Christ, who is God over all, forever praised," the footnote offers two alternative readings, both of which remove the Deity of Christ from the verse entirely. So, what is not twisted in the text or removed altogether, is all too often damaged by a footnote. Whichever method they choose, it all accomplishes the same. Heresies flourish in conditions like these.

Where the centurion confessed in Mark 15:39 that Jesus "was the Son of God," the footnote suggests that the words "the Son," could have been "a son." The same footnote is found for Matt. 27:54. Needless to say, such fumbling with the truth neither enhances the student's reading of the Bible, nor edifies their life in the least. The only thing it ever accomplishes is eternal damage to the soul. It should have certainly occurred to the author of this footnote that if the centurion had been so misinformed as to have called Jesus "a son of God," when He is not identified by such a title anywhere else in Scripture, his words would not have been worth recording in even one book of the Bible, let alone in the two in which they are found. Hence, this footnote questions nothing but itself.

Dear reader, none of this should ever be taken lightly. Whether these footnotes are casting serious doubts on key texts or not, they unsettle the faith of the reader and keep him in a continual state of doubt. And the more one loves the Bible, the more deeply he feels the pain. God's Word is supposed to be our final authority; but how can it be in confusion like this?

Not to be limited to the bottom of the page, the translators of the NIV have also printed their notes in the text itself—between the verses. For instance, after reading Mark 16:8, the reader is interrupted by a black line and then a note that is printed just before verse 9. This note strongly suggests (on the authority of other manuscripts) that the next twelve verses might not have appeared in the original Scriptures, in spite of all of the evidence to the contrary. Consequently, the force of this powerful passage and its relevance to our lives is lost. A personal acquaintance told me that after he read this note in Mark 16, his faith in the Bible was so shattered that he did not know what to believe any more. Fellow Christian, when it comes to the Bible, our guiding rule must always be, "let God be true, but every man a liar" (Rom. 3:4).

A similar note is found in John 7, between verses 52 and 53. This note implies that the next twelve verses that tell the story of the woman caught in adultery (John 7:53-8:11) are not authentic either. Which, of course, perpetually casts irreparable suspicion over one of the most cherished and widely acclaimed stories in the Bible.

How low has our estimation of the Bible sunk and our pride in scholastic achievement risen that we would dare soil the Scriptures this way. These numerous notes, all worthless in themselves, cause even the most committed believer to question whether he has God's Word or, at best, men's opinion of what it is. How can a minister preach with conviction "Thus saith the Lord," when the very Bible he uses keeps reminding him that he cannot be sure God said it?

While only time can fully assess all of the damage being done here, in the meantime, let us not overlook the obvious. To any sensible man, saved or otherwise, the NIV makes today's Bible look like a blunderous effort to piece together what is hopefully left of the Word of God.

SOME BACKGROUND ON THE CORRUPTED MANUSCRIPTS

Without the aid of modern printing that enables us today to reproduce literature perfectly, the ancients had to reproduce all of their literature through handwritten copy. Moreover, since all written material wears out with age until it finally becomes unusable, scribes of old had to recopy their documents often in order to pass them down through the centuries to our generation. So, naturally, the further a piece of literature dated back, the more often it needed recopying.

Now this work was taxing and beset with problems. Due to copyist errors, occasional damaged or lost pages, readers' marginal notations that might have been mistakenly included into a text, etc., an original work could incur a great deal of change and damage over the passing of time. Consequently, upon its arrival today, we could never expect it to be in its original form.

Since our Bible also is extremely old and had to pass through countless hands to arrive at this hour, it is generally supposed that it too suffered damage and cannot be found presently in its purest original form. In an attempt to correct this problem, the science of textual criticism was developed. This is a procedure that generally appoints biased scholars to estimate the extent of this damage and then supervise the repair.

However, we are not dealing now with just another piece of ancient literature written by men that would have to depend upon men to survive. This is the crowned monarch of all literature that was produced supernaturally by the inspiration of God and that can depend upon God for its keeping.

Knowing how limited and incompetent even the most qualified of men would be, God had no intention of trusting the keeping of His Word with us. As was stated earlier, our part in its preservation is to leave it alone and pass it on, in tact, to the next generation. To guard it against accidents and any natural forces that would come against it, would be God's responsibility, and He said so. The Psalmist, for example, was inspired to write: "The words of the Lord are pure words:..Thou shalt keep them, O Lord, thou shalt preserve them from this generation for ever" (Ps. 12:6, 7).

The Bible's eternal permanence was also guaranteed in Isa.

40:8: "the word of our God shall stand for ever." This promise is repeated in 1 Pet. 1:25 to show that it stood for the New Testament as well as it did for the Old Testament.

In Matt. 24:35, Christ declared: "Heaven and earth shall pass away, but my words shall not pass away." Thus, we can expect creation to disappear before even one line disappears from off of the Bible page.

Now these promises should have been more than enough to convince even the most doubtful skeptic that the God Who produced the Bible would Himself preserve it—that as it had been Divinely authored, so would it be Divinely kept. However, to their shame, they were not convinced, and without faith enough to believe that what God had promised He could also perform, set out with enough faith in themselves to perform it for Him.

"But why," one might ask, "are there so many flaws in the Bible?" There are no flaws in the Bible; at least not in the preserved Word of God as it is found in the Traditional Text from which the King James Version was translated. In this Bible, we can put our total confidence, having first put our faith in God, Who made the promises we just considered.

"But why," another might question, "can't we put that same faith in the other translations?" While it is apparent that the Church today has two different sets of Scripture, it should be equally as apparent that God did not write both. When a study is made of the history of the Bible, it becomes clear that the scores of omissions and alterations found in modern translations were not the result of careless copy making over the centuries but of an intentional plot to destroy God's Word—and, therefore, its readers as well.

"If this is all true, why then," you ask, "do a lot of good men today prefer, for example, the NIV to the KJV?" Good men have stood on both sides of every issue the Church has ever dealt with. However, if good men preferring the NIV is (for some Christians) a gauge to measure spiritual reliability, this also should be pointed out: Some of the most notable heretics of the past, ever to attack pure doctrine, were not only responsible for authoring the omissions and changes found in the NIV but also with establishing them in the text. A look at the origin and history of the manuscripts the NIV was based upon and the questionable crowd that surrounded them, is as shocking as our comparative look at its text.

Let us look briefly at the history of these blemished manuscripts. The learned Dr. Scrivener supplies the key to our understanding of this subject in the following: "The worst corruptions to which the New Testament has ever been subjected, originated within a hundred years after it was composed."[2]

Actually, this work had begun at the earliest possible stage. In fact, evidence shows that while the Scriptures were being authored, plans were being laid to destroy them. Paul testified to this early activity when he wrote to the Corinthians in about A.D. 58, "For we are not as many, which corrupt the word of God" (2 Cor. 2:17). Then around A.D. 66, Peter wrote, while making reference to Paul's writings, "in which are some things hard to be understood, which they that are unlearned and unstable wrest, as they do also the other scriptures, unto their own destruction" (2 Pet. 3:16). The word "wrest" [Greek: strebloo] means to twist, to torture—and this Peter confirmed was being done to the Scriptures. While the Church was still in its infancy, a heretical group was twisting God's Word into an entirely different meaning.

How did this all come about? During the last half of the first century, a belief system called Gnosticism had begun to develop in the Church. This was an attempt to produce a successful philosophy, by mixing previously failed philosophies with the spiritual disciplines of the new religion. Now, when one becomes a Christian, they must relinquish their old concepts of both the spiritual and the natural and learn afresh as the Holy Spirit guides them into all truth. Gnostics, however, were not willing to do this. Among the assortment of views they had pledged themselves to keep was the unfounded idea that all physical matter was inherently evil—which, naturally, left them confused as to how a good God could have manifested Himself in evil flesh.

Void of God's Spirit and quite on their own, the Gnostics attempted to harmonize this error with what was clearly opposing them in Scripture. Unable to accomplish this, they eventually settled on several theories that contradicted the Scriptures outrightly. Some taught that Christ had no body at all but that He was, in fact, a phantom. Others taught that He had a type of nonmaterial body. And still others taught that Jesus and Christ were two separate entities. The latter believed that Christ was the power that descended upon the man Jesus at His baptism, only to leave Him again just prior to His death.

With such error at the base, it became necessary for the Gnostics to construct an entirely new religion. As they re-defined the Scriptures –propping each lie against the truth upon the framework of another– an alternative "faith" was made available to the Church, with a number of doctrinal changes.

As Christians began to explore the heresy, the clear revelation of Jesus given to them in Scripture became so confused that the Apostles themselves were forced to address the whole business in writing. Sparing neither the feelings nor the words, John branded all Gnostics "antichrist" and clearly saw them as forerunners of "the" Antichrist. "Little children, it is the last time: and as ye have heard that antichrist shall come, even now are there many antichrists; whereby we know that it is the last time. They went out from us, but they were not of us...Beloved, believe not every spirit, but try the spirits whether they are of God: because many false prophets are gone out into the world. Hereby know ye the Spirit of God: Every spirit that confesseth that Jesus Christ is come in the flesh is of God: And every spirit that confesseth not that Jesus Christ is come in the flesh is not of God: and this is that spirit of antichrist, whereof ye have heard that it should come; and even now already is it in the world" (1 John 2:18, 19; 4:1-3).

Gnosticism was not the outcome of a sincere albeit misguided search for truth, but of a deliberate departure from it—whose chief ambition was to convert Christianity into just another pagan philosophy. It was Satan's attempt not only to shatter the truth about Jesus Christ but, it would appear from John's writings, that Gnosticism would also serve as a support base upon which Satan, in time, could effectively position the Antichrist. It might be interesting for the reader to reexamine the New Testament while keeping in mind the presence of the Gnostics and their teachings in the early Church.

When the Apostles died, the Gnostics (along with other heretical factions) began making their most serious moves. In an effort to weaken their greatest remaining obstacle, the Bible, they began to rewrite it—and, apparently, without fear or conscience. To accommodate their mistaken ideas about Jesus and His doctrine, they added freely to the Scriptures and whatever truth they disagreed with was removed by the stroke of a pen. Eusebius, in Ecclesiastical History, LCS, Vol. 1, pp. 522-524, quoted another, who during the second century wrote: "Wherefore, they have not fear to lay hands on the divine Scriptures under pretense of correcting them...As for their denying their guilt, the thing is impossible, since the copies were written in their own hand; and they did not receive the Scriptures in this condition from their teachers, nor can they show the originals from which they made their copies."[3]

While there are those who speak highly of such second century fathers as Justin Martyr, Tatian, and Clement of Alexandria, there are others who find very little to commend them for since each of these, in their turn, contributed to this corruption of Scripture.

Perhaps the man who did the most, however, to blend the Scriptures with Gnosticism was Origen (185-254 A.D.). Also, to his discredit, no one ever championed more apostate teachings that found a permanent place in history, than he. Yet, his influence upon Christianity, from his day to ours, can hardly be measured by words. Not only did his ideas captivate the attention of the Catholic Church forever, but also nearly all of the Protestant scholars of this century have been swayed by the power of this one man's thinking. While his genius and insight into the Scriptures were extraordinary, his preference for

Gnosticism, Platonism, Mysticism, and the early heresies made him anything but a safe guide or teacher. His doctrines were repulsive. Though considered the greatest theologian of the third century, he taught that stars have souls, devils would be saved, and such errors as purgatory and transubstantiation. He also taught (through his application of the Greek) that Jesus was created and did not eternally exist as God. Little wonder why such a man would have said: "The Scriptures are of little use to those who understand them as they are written."[4]

Origen deliberately changed the Scriptures to suit his own confused philosophy and, in the process, made many of the deletions we now find in modern translations of the Bible. It was Origen who mightily influenced Jerome (about 340-420 A.D.) who translated the Latin Vulgate which was made the official Bible of the Catholic Church by the Council of Trent in 1546. And it was Origen again who was to play such a large role in the affairs of twentieth century Protestantism, as we will see in the following.

When Constantine (280?-337 A.D.) became the Emperor of Rome, he endeavored to form a union between Christianity and paganism. Since Origen had successfully blended Christianity with pagan philosophy, Constantine commissioned Eusebius, a great admirer of Origen, to prepare fifty Bibles based upon Origen's corrupted Scriptures for use in the churches.

Skipping past many centuries filled with attacks upon the true Word of God and persecution of its followers, we come to the year 1481 A.D. In this year a very old manuscript (Codex Vaticanus) was discovered lying dormant on a shelf of the Vatican library. Then in 1844,* another old manuscript (Codex Sinaiticus) was discovered in a wastebasket in St. Catherine's monastery at the foot of Mt. Sinai. Both of these manuscripts, Vaticanus and Sinaiticus, date back to the time Eusebius produced those fifty Bibles for Constantine and are believed by many to be survivors of that lot.

Here, is where the drama begins to really unfold. In the year 1853 two Cambridge professors, Brooke Foss Westcott and Fenton John Anthony Hort (better known as Westcott and Hort), began preparing a Greek text based primarily on the Vaticanus and Sinaiticus manuscripts.

Now, when the student arrives at the subject of Westcott and Hort, he should not pass too quickly. Because it was through these men that our long link to the apostate past was connected. Westcott and Hort, who might well be called the "intellectual descendants of the ancient heretics," with skill and great subtlety, delivered to the Church of the twentieth century, the religion of their fathers.

Let us, for a moment, pay them the attention they deserve.

---

*Actually, the "Sinaiticus" was discovered in part in 1844 and in its entirety in 1859.

Though they were masters of communication and hardly rivaled for their knowledge; their scholarship nevertheless, was strikingly outweighed by their theological ineptness. Neither Westcott nor Hort ever stated that the Bible was verbally inspired or inerrant. On the other hand, while Hort praised in writing Darwin's theory of evolution and seriously questioned whether Eden ever existed; Westcott, in his writings, flatly denied the Genesis account of Creation. To put it in his own words, "No one now, I suppose, holds that the first three chapters of Genesis, for example, give a literal history—I could never understand how any one reading them with open eyes could think they did."[5]

Also, though Protestants would prefer to think otherwise, Westcott and Hort gave almost every indication of being Catholics under cover. As a case in point, they seemed equally as comfortable worshipping Jesus or Mary. "I have been persuaded for many years (Hort wrote) that Mary-worship and 'Jesus'-worship have very much in common in their causes and their results."[6] (Notice, he had held this opinion "many years.") Concerning a statue of Mary and a crucified Christ that Westcott happened on in a remote little chapel, he wrote: "Had I been alone I could have knelt there for hours."[7] And, to prove that his reverence for Mary, like Hort's, was no passing fancy, he also wrote some eighteen years latter, "I wish I could see to what forgotten truth Mariolatry bears witness."[8]

Westcott and Hort's preference for Catholic dogma was evident elsewhere as well. While Hort, for example, felt it proper to call the doctrine of Evangelicals "perverted,"[9] he revealed his own perverse creed by proudly calling himself a "staunch sacerdotalist."[10] This is one who requires a priest to mediate between himself and his Divine needs, or one who cannot spiritually function without the authority of the priesthood. It is easy to understand, then, why one of Hort's stated concerns was that "Protestants unlearn the crazy horror of the idea of priesthood."[11]

Revealing more of the dark side of his convictions, Hort also warned, "We dare not forsake the sacraments or God will forsake us."[12] The sacraments are, of course, what all good Catholics are never to forsake.

Now, if there remains any doubt as to which side of the fence both Westcott and Hort stood on, the following should settle the matter. Hort wrote to Westcott, "Protestantism is only parenthetical and temporary."[13] Hort also wrote to John Ellerton, "The pure Romish view seems to me nearer, and more likely to lead to the truth than the Evangelical."[14]

Such was the man who also dared to put in writing: "The popular doctrine of substitution is an immoral and material counterfeit...Certainly nothing could be more unscriptural than the modern limiting of Christ's bearing our sins and sufferings to his death; but indeed that is only one aspect of an almost universal heresy." [15]

It actually puts a strain upon the mind to realize that these are the men who not only produced the Greek text that modern Bibles are based upon, but also invented all of the reasons why the Church today should no longer rely on the true text.

What took place after Westcott and Hort finished their text was nothing less than outrageous. In one of the most infamous moments in Church history, the Vaticanus and Sinaiticus (by way of the Westcott and Hort Greek text) were slipped into the hands of liberal theologians who, in the latter part of the nineteenth century, convinced the Protestants that these very old manuscripts were, in fact, the real Scriptures. One theologian after another succumbed to the lie and have been translating Bibles from them ever since. All of which causes Christians today to mistakenly assume that for the greater part of Church history (around 1550 years since the writing of the Vaticanus and Sinaiticus) Christianity was without the real Word of God, until it was recently reintroduced in our modern translations, the first of which was the Revised Version of 1881.

This, then, is the history behind our modern translations of the Bible. To sum it all up in a line: From the ancient Gnostics to Westcott and Hort, like a product passed through the skillful hands of an assembly line, a new set of Scriptures had been developed.

There are those who, while unable to disprove this evidence, nevertheless, insist that no matter what transpired years ago, the Church today is far too knowledgeable to have in its possession Scriptures that are flawed. But consider this: If within a scarce sixty years or so of the day of Pentecost, the Church of Pergamos could have the doctrine of Balaam; the Church of Thyatira, a Jezebel for both prophetess and teacher; the Church of Sardis, a name that it lived but was dead; and the Church of Laodicea, such a lukewarm spirit that Christ had threatened to vomit it out of His mouth, is it too hard to believe that the Church, some nineteen hundred years later, could have a corrupted set of Scriptures?

We do well to remember that the first apostasy took place in Heaven, in the very presence of God Himself, when Lucifer turned a myriad of angels against Him. Should we be surprised then to witness this defection from truth in His Church

~ ~ ~ ~ ~ ~ ~ ~ ~ ~ ~ ~

For a point of interest: In 1853 Westcott and Hort began preparing their Greek text. Interestingly, six years later Darwin published his *Origin of Species*. Consider the parallel: As the world was being offered an entirely new science, the Church was being furnished with an entirely new Bible. A coincidence? Not at all. It was all part of a Satanic strategy. Both works have done such damage to humanity that only the return of Jesus can repair it.

~ ~ ~ ~ ~ ~ ~ ~ ~ ~ ~ ~

All of man's attempts to impair God's Word, however, could not keep God from preserving it. By an act of Divine Grace, the greatest group of Bible scholars ever assembled in the history of the Church went to work and produced the finest translation of the Bible in history—the King James Version. Contrary to what many are led to believe, corrupted manuscripts from which modern Bibles are translated, were available to them as well—however, they refused to employ them. The text base they selected for the King James Version was the Traditional Text, which had also been employed by the father of the Protestant Reformation, Martin Luther.

We may assume that their reasons for choosing the Traditional Text were basic. It had been the preferred text of the Church from the beginning. Approximately ninety per cent of all of the surviving Greek manuscripts agreed with it. Also, its history had continued from faith to faith, while the others had journeyed from conspiracy, through corruption, to chaos. Its providential story, and of how God kept His Word on its perilous journey over the passage of time, is thoroughly covered in many fine books that are available to the Church today.

Since God has promised to preserve His Word, we have to believe that it is out there somewhere. Furthermore, since it was written to be consulted by men that it would naturally be found throughout Church History, in the general use of God's people—as we find was the case of the Traditional Text, from which the King James Version was translated. It would not be found in a manuscript collecting dust in the Vatican library, or in a manuscript assigned to a wastepaper basket in a secluded monastery, or in still others of equally suspicious origin—all of which furnished the text base for the NIV and other modern translations of the Bible.

~ ~ ~ ~ ~ ~ ~ ~ ~ ~ ~ ~

However, not all believe that God kept His promise to preserve His Word and because we do have conflicting sets of Scripture today, they believe they must assist God, in putting it all back right again. Unfortunately, however, their attempt to accomplish this has bred even bigger problems than those they proposed to solve. For example, Paul tells us, "faith cometh by hearing, and hearing by the word of God"; which, naturally, means that we must have faith in God's Word, to have faith in

Him. Yet, modern textual critics would have us postpone our faith in God's Word until they can satisfy themselves that it is God's Word. Which, of course, only prolongs the process that now goes something like this:

(1) We must first put our faith in our scholar friends
(2) who will tell us where and when to put our faith in the Bible
(3) that will encourage our faith in God
(4) Who alone can provide salvation and all of our spiritual needs.

So, to have an absolute faith in God, we will first need to have an absolute faith in men. Before we can rest upon God's Word, they will have to shore up its foundations. Which, of course, is a feat they have not yet accomplished and one that every discerning saint knows, they never will. How does one solve a problem that, in reality, does not exist?

Also, not to be overlooked, when it becomes apparent to the Christian that his Bible is often the product of opinion, he most naturally concludes that he is entitled to his own opinion. Who says he cannot have "his religion" his way. Should we be surprised then to see such rife independence in the Church today, besides all that came with it: rock music, alcohol, depraved morals, and every other deviation from truth the carnal mind can concoct? In the absence of a sure Bible, who can insist upon a sure religion? If, in their opinion, God did not see fit to pass on to our generation, through unblemished Scriptures, His final authority, who then can have it?

Regretfully, all of this promises to get worse. In fact, the current efforts to put into the hands of the next generation these corrupted Scriptures, and to leave that generation absent of any written witness to the truth, is alarming. How are they planning to accomplish this? Through the reeducation of God's people. They are making it popular to believe that if you are a Bible authority you must stand with them; and further, that all dissenters are divisive. In what better way can the enemies of the Bible bring down the Bible than by pretending to be its experts. Now, while this has always been their strategy, they have never had more success at it than they are having today. Seminaries have been prepared and countless scholars recruited. Their deception is as firmly entrenched in the Church of this century as the theory of evolution is in the world of science. And not only is it perilous to try to expose it, but also you are generally ridiculed for not also believing the lie. Nevertheless, while they strain to stamp out every syllable of truth and gather a million authorities to hail their lie, God's Word, according to His own promise, will not be destroyed!

~ ~ ~ ~ ~ ~ ~ ~ ~ ~ ~ ~

Let us be reminded: (1) When the world had finally climbed out of the Dark Ages and into the light of the Protestant Reformation; (2) when the printing press had been invented and Bibles were being produced in large quantities, and (3) when God especially used the English speaking people during those spiritually great centuries of missionary work and evangelization, it was with the Traditional Text and the King James Version based upon that text that God chose to accomplish His mighty work. When the Church experienced a sort of golden age and achieved an excellence that later Christianity has looked back upon in wonder, this was the Bible that God placed into the hands of many of the most powerful ministers, missionaries, and evangelists the forces of Hell have ever encountered. IT WAS NOT THE TEXT BASE THAT MODERN BIBLES ARE TRANSLATED FROM, but the Traditional Text that had stood the test of the centuries.

When that light began to dim, though, and the world entered an even darker age, during which Christians no longer endured "sound doctrine," as the Holy Spirit warned but turned "away...from the truth" and gave heed instead "to seducing spirits, and doctrines of devils," it was then that these modern Bibles arrived to complement the chaos—and to confuse, corrupt, and catholicize, if they could, every Born Again Christian on earth.

~ ~ ~ ~ ~ ~ ~ ~ ~ ~ ~ ~

As a careful student traces the history of the Bible in any honest source of reference, he can easily discern the presence of Catholicism. Though dimmed in the shadows, it was nevertheless there—intriguing, maneuvering, and exerting all means to bring down Christianity through the sabotage of Scripture. Can there be any doubt then why, where modern translations of the Bible go the Roman Catholic Church follows? Observe the many big name Christians today as well as whole Protestant denominations that are eager to fellowship with the Catholic Church. Not only do they labor together in spiritual and civil matters, from protesting abortion to joint efforts to supposedly reach the lost, but also they engage in open dialogue to find common ground upon which to blend their theologies. Now, while most prefer to look the other way, or pretend that it is not as wrong as it obviously is, remember—there are none so blind as those who refuse to see.

Dear reader, it is only the most willfully ignorant who do not recognize by now that all roads lead to Rome—where all doors are kept open to whichever hapless religion might wander in. Culturally able to overlap any people, her highways extend to all places. The Roman Catholic Church cuts deep into the Orient where, with her mystical side, she allures. She penetrates the jungle where, with her masteries in idolatry, she can entice even the most bedeviled minds. Some come by way of her philosophical appeal, while others come up the steeper slopes of her political preeminence. Yet, the best maintained of all her highways are those that cut across Protestant paths. Upon these she sings songs about Jesus and waves to those lost sheep who strayed from her fold so long ago. Hence, as Protestants lose their adoption and Catholics put on the "appearance," they each move steadily toward the middle, where a simple readjustment of differences makes them all ONE again.

~ ~ ~ ~ ~ ~ ~ ~ ~ ~ ~ ~ ~

Regarding the Church's preoccupation with New Age phenomenon, consider the following thoughts. Here we will see where contemporary Bibles are taking the Church.

New Age philosophy offers the quickest route away from God that, perhaps, men have ever taken. In an amazingly short time, multitudes have gone from simple religion to a complex worship of the creation and self. While modern translations of the Bible are not New Age in doctrine, they are in nature—their agendas complement. They labor as "one" to blend the Church and world together. As New Age thinking embraces anything but Jesus, these new translations lead the Church further and further from Him. While the secular is militant and openly brash, the religious succeeds through conspiracy and fraud. Is there an objective in view? Rev. 13:3-8 holds the answer. All of the religious and nonreligious people of society will gather as one, to worship Satan and the Antichrist. Farfetched? Study hard the thirteenth chapter of Revelation. Something causes everyone to worship them. As the world's loudest voice, secular New Ageism, prepares the lost; the Church's most certain voice, God's Bible (distorted through modern translations), prepares its own.

May the reader be reminded that much of what is wrong with modern Bibles can be traced back to the ancient Gnostics who, according to the Scriptures, prefigured the Antichrist. Thus, the Gnostics, Origen, Constantine, Westcott, Hort, Antichrist, and many lesser names between are synonymous. They all contributed to a "Satanic Masterpiece."

—First, the Gnostics and Origen blended the Scriptures with the pagan's view of Christ.

—Then Constantine, with the aid of these Scriptures, blended Christianity with paganism.

—Currently, with these same Scriptures, numerous Church leaders and theologians, under the delusion of Westcott and Hort, are blending Protestantism with Catholicism.

—Which, next, will be blended with every other religion.

—And then, finally, with the pagan world, in a One World

Empire under a One World Emperor.

While some might call it foolish to suggest that these Scriptures alone are responsible for this, it would be even more foolish to suggest that they are not an enormous contributing factor—if not, in fact, the sole contributing factor.

Reader, I encourage you to examine the history of the Bible for yourself. You will not miss finding unmistakable evidence of a plot against the Bible and, accordingly, the Church. If we genuinely fear displeasing God and know how serious a matter the Scriptures are to Him, we will not want to be found standing on the wrong side of this issue before the judgment seat of Christ.

~ ~ ~ ~ ~ ~ ~ ~ ~ ~ ~ ~

Actually, this practice of corrupting Scripture, and subsequently God's people, goes all of the way back to the Garden of Eden. Although Adam and Eve did not have much of God's Word, what little they had, Satan went after. His first words to Eve were, "Yea, hath God said?" Once Eve was sufficiently shaken by the question posed and began to doubt God's Word, Satan's second step was to outrightly deny God's Word. Though God had warned, concerning the forbidden tree, "in the day that thou eatest thereof thou shalt surely die," Satan contradicted Him by saying "Ye shall not surely die." Shortly afterward, the fatal bite was taken.

His strategy has not changed; it is as cunning as it is lethal and remains the same to this day. He begins by destroying faith in the Word of God and, once this is accomplished, replaces it with his own.

In looking back at the fall, we can see that neither Adam nor Eve accepted the entire Word of God. They clung to what was pleasant and permissible, "Of every tree of the garden thou mayest freely eat." Yet, they rejected the prohibition, "of the tree of the knowledge of good and evil, thou shalt not eat of it."

How different was the case of Jesus (the last Adam), Who was not in a garden paradise when He encountered the enemy but in the wilderness and was not fat and full but, after fasting for forty days, was nothing but skin and bones. Yet, we find Him declaring to Satan, who also tempted Him with food, "Man shall not live by bread alone, but by EVERY word that proceedeth out of the mouth of God."

Adam and Eve picked and chose over the words of God, but to Jesus "EVERY" word of God was important. If we truly believe that they are God's words, then they are not to be regarded lightly. If Jesus refused to do such a thing, how much more should we?

CURRENT INDIFFERENCE

God's Word is not to be trifled with, especially when it is dealing with the crucial subject of the Lord Jesus Christ. Yet, in spite of its shameful attacks upon the Person and work of Jesus, some not only prefer the NIV, but also will vigorously defend it on every ground. It is a strange philosophy, indeed, that persuades a Christian to be more loyal to a book that dishonors his Lord than he is to his Lord.

It should be mentioned here, for the benefit of all readers, that most modern translations of the Bible are generally as inaccurate as the NIV though not always in the same places. To see this for yourself, compare your version of the Bible with the King James Version in each of the verse comparisons found on pages 3 through 65. The results, I assure you, will be disturbing.

While the corruption in modern translations has to be exposed, it is doubtful the information will be received by all. In fact, what is nearly as incredible as this molestation of Scripture, is the willingness of a lot of Christians today to sit back and accept it all without raising so much as an eyebrow. When shown these discrepancies, they prefer to side step the issue rather than to admit that we have a problem. I suppose if some can excuse everything from the inquisition of the past to rosary beads in Christian book stores today, they can excuse this as well—and in fact have.

For example, some excuse the omission of words, statements, and whole verses, by claiming that the reader can assume what truths are missing, even in their absence. However, this could only be true if there were a higher written authority than the Bible to turn to. We might assume an author's intention if key words were left out of some other Christian book—but not from the Bible that furnishes all of the facts and information upon which we base our assumptions. How can a truth be assumed if it is not in the very Book that supplies us our truth?

Others defend the inaccuracies in modern versions of the Bible with this appeal: "Let's stick to where our Bibles agree rather than quarrel over where they disagree." "After all," they tell us, "since so much of any modern translation is accurate and only a small portion inaccurate, we don't really have cause for alarm."

I wonder if these Christians take the same attitude with their health. Could they reasonably say for instance: "Ninety per cent of me is in perfect health. I do, however, have a little cancer developing that threatens my life but why should I worry, the rest of me is in great shape." Now, that makes no sense at all, does it. Neither does the idea that error should be condoned because it is found within the company of so much that is correct. Error is error, and even the smallest one permits no amount of right answers to produce a perfect score.

Though the following is crude, allow it to make a point.

The greater part of rat poison is nutritional. If the rat were fed that much alone it would remain quite healthy. But that is not all that the manufacturer's of the poison feed it. In fact, they have no desire to make any wholesome contribution to the rat at all. Their desire, as you know, is to kill it. Accordingly, if even ninety per cent of a modern translation were accurate that should make it, for the discerning Christian, all the more dangerous. Because, like the rat poison, it is simply an elaborate cover up of the deadly.

No one opposed to modern translations of the Bible fails to see that the real Word of God can be found in these Bibles and, indeed, in great supply. They are simply opposed, as any Christian should be, to the thousands upon thousands of omissions, word replacements, and paraphrases that are found in these versions, as well as the many personal interpretations that have been woven into God's Word—of which the NIV, in every one of these areas, is a classic example.

Getting back to the omissions again, some defend them by pointing out that while a text might be missing from one place in Scripture, it is sometimes found somewhere else in Scripture. In other words, in some cases, essential writings were not removed from all passages. "So," they exclaim, "what is all of this fuss about?" Beyond question, this has to be one of the most reckless attitudes toward Scripture in the Church, and can only belong to those so dulled by compromise and backslidden in heart that they have lost all sense of reality. The Bible is not simply another publication out there on the open market of religious books. It is the very Word of God, which God deliberately placed above His own name (Ps. 138:2), and of which even He Himself, will not alter one word (Ps. 89:34). How then can a God fearing Christian justify, even the slightest omission from its page? Are they not as much as saying that men have as much right to discard Scriptures as God did to write them down?

To justify an omission because it can be found somewhere else does not answer the question of why it was removed in the first place. Instead, such sleight of hand reasoning openly insults the declared infallibility of God's Holy Word, creates alibis for its corrupters, and instructs the saints that they can live without all of God's counsel. It plainly lowers the Bible in status to just "another book" that we can do with as we please.

However, while the Church's tolerance for blemished Scripture is high—God's is not. If He forbids, under the severest penalty, the adding or taking away of a single word of Scripture in Rev. 22:18, 19,* will He be lenient with those who support translations that have clearly tampered with the Scriptures? Or, will they stand as guilty on the day of judgment for their rationalizing, as the ones who did the tampering in the first place.

Satan does not have to do much from without when such indifference lies within. It is this very spirit of nonresistance that the spoilers of God's Word had hoped for and that will encourage them to do even further damage to Scripture. With the unchangeable Word of God now subject to the changeable views of men, what will the next generation of Bibles be like? If we today are willing to give up our most for less, will saints of tomorrow be willing to give up this less for nothing? Surely, paganism lies at the door. The world and the Church are making a full circle back to the years that preceded the cross; when men, like Pilate, will have to ask once again, "What is truth?" May God help us!

~ ~ ~ ~ ~ ~ ~ ~ ~ ~ ~ ~

Here are just a few practical reasons why words should never be taken from the Bible:

(1) Some people never form the habit of searching the Scriptures and often limit their awareness of an entire truth to a single verse of Scripture. Perhaps for this reason, a key teaching is often repeated several times in the Bible. In this way, even the casual reader is bound to happen upon it once. We see an example of this in the four Gospels; particularly Matthew, Mark, and Luke, which essentially retell the same story of the life of Christ. Certainly, this type of reader has a better chance of finding what he needs in the KJV than he does in the NIV. Those important words, for example, in Matt. 9:13 that were omitted from the NIV, he might never discover in Luke 5:32 of the NIV, where they were not omitted.

(2) An important truth gathers force as it is retold over the pages of Scripture and becomes less likely to be forgotten. Contrariwise, to remove it here and there accomplishes the opposite.

(3) If the day ever comes when Bibles are confiscated and we have to divide and share a surviving Bible, so that all can have a portion of God's Word, what truths will be lost if the Bible is the NIV? That precious truth, for instance, that was torn out in Matt. 9:13 but left in its place in Luke 5:32, is lost forever to the one who only has Matt. 9:13.

---

*While the warnings in Rev. 22:18, 19 are addressed to the writing of Revelation, their placement at the very close of the Bible has led some to view them as having a dual role. As applying specifically to Revelation and, in principle, to the whole Bible. See also Deut. 4:2; 12:32; Prov. 30:6.

(4) Lastly, God honors His Word and through it—its readers. It is a perfect piece of literature. Consequently, any deletion or word change (irrespective of the thousands found in the NIV) damages the whole and the Bible becomes less than perfect. Its instructions to our lives then, will become less than perfect. Our lives as well will fall far short of the mark. And our hope in Christ will become anything but certain.

Again, we have neither the right to tamper with Scripture nor to regard such tamperings as the Word of God. With Heaven and Hell awaiting the outcome of all of our lives, a Christian's loyalty to Jesus must exceed his loyalty to what professes to be a Bible.

~ ~ ~ ~ ~ ~ ~ ~ ~ ~ ~ ~ ~

Some claim that words, lines, and whole verses were not taken out of the original Scriptures but, in fact, added in. Therefore, they believe that the KJV, rather than the modern translations, fell victim to the corrupters. Their argument, however, has been answered by both history and common sense. It has never been the practice of the corrupters of God's Word to enhance the doctrine of Christ: to make it both fuller and richer as we find it in the KJV. Furthermore, early Church Fathers had quoted many of these texts in their writings long before they were supposedly added in. Then, of course, there is that awesome statistic the opposition seems to want to forget: Approximately ninety per cent of the more than five thousand ancient Greek manuscripts now in custody agree with the KJV!

However, the most destructive blow to their theory (that these additional readings in the KJV were not found in the original manuscripts) can be seen in the following: Wilbur Pickering observed that Westcott and Hort, in their effort to explain where these readings originated, "invented history." [16] They alleged that a council of church leaders had gathered centuries ago for the express purpose of adding additional contents to the Scriptures. And yet, history offers us no evidence at all that such a council ever existed or that such an undertaking ever took place. Burgon, one of the finest textual scholars of the last century, stated, "Apart however from the gross intrinsic improbability of the supposed Recension, [i.e. a critical revision of a text] the utter absence of one particle of evidence, traditional or otherwise, that it ever did take place, must be held to be fatal to the hypotheses that it did. It is simply incredible that an incident of such magnitude and interest would leave no trace of itself in history." [17]

Over against this myth, what significant proof do we have that these additional readings are authentic? Portions of second century manuscripts have been discovered that contain many of the additional readings found currently in the KJV. Readings that modern critics assured us, in the true spirit of Westcott and

Hort, were added centuries later. And yet, here they are found in the very oldest manuscripts unearthed to date. Now, in view of these monumental discoveries, one should expect the opposition to concede their case, admit their error, and come over to the side of God's infallible Word. Yet, the very opposite has taken place. These hirelings in our system continue to teach their lies in spite of these historic breakthroughs. I suppose, though, that this is what we should have expected. In fact, it appears to be the accepted practice of most of the Church today to ignore this evidence along with the rest of the evidence that continues to come in in support of the KJV.

A minister once told me that a familiar enemy on occasion can be a whole lot easier to get along with than an unfamiliar friend. This can certainly be evidenced here. The lie has become so much a part of our lives and our theology that there is no room left for the truth. We have built our religion, our resources, and our hopes upon the "lie" and are now too fearful to live without it. We are actually now in the same contemptible state as every other heretical faction, from the ancient Arians to the modern Laodiceans, whose deceptive ways we despise.

~ ~ ~ ~ ~ ~ ~ ~ ~ ~ ~ ~

"But does it all really matter," one might ask, "if I can support what I believe with the NIV?" Yes, if someone else can refute what you believe with that same translation. While you could prove, for example, the Deity of Jesus by using the NIV, someone else can disprove His Deity by using the NIV. While you could prove the virgin birth with this translation, another could disprove it with this same translation—whichever be their pleasure. The NIV is clearly an "Interdenominational Masterpiece" that can cross any church threshold and make all within happy with whatever they believe. A remarkable illustration of this can be seen in the following:

Perhaps there is no religious movement less respected by Born Again Christians than the religion of the Jehovah's Witnesses. Furthermore, there is no version of the Bible less cared for by Christians than the Jehovah's Witness Bible, the New World Translation. However, if a Jehovah's Witness were to exchange his Bible, the New World Translation, for the NIV, he would find it surprisingly much to his liking. Consider for example these facts: In this book, we looked at 147 places in the KJV where words or whole verses were omitted in the NIV.* Of these 147 omissions, 146 of them ARE ALSO OMITTED IN THE JEHOVAH'S WITNESS BIBLE. If you were to add to these

---

*These 147 omissions also include the (Compare also) verses that were not written out in the verse comparisons.

omissions all of the word changes found in the NIV that have been noted in this book, you would find the Jehovah's Witness Bible and the NIV in agreement IN BETTER THAN FOURTEEN OUT OF EVERY FIFTEEN CASES.*

In fact, some Jehovah's Witnesses have found the NIV so much to their liking that a minister told me that, on one occasion, he observed them using it while witnessing. Why members of an organization so void of the truth and bent on destroying the Deity of Jesus would use the NIV certainly demands an explanation from somebody!

Something to ponder: I do not know of one Christian who uses a New World Translation nor have I ever heard that such a Christian exists. Have you? Yet, the NIV, whose contents so closely resemble those of the New World Translation, is the best selling Bible in the English speaking world today. If that is not a paradox, what is?

---

*This does not include the list of names and titles on page 66.

CONCLUSION

At the very root of the Church's problems today, lie these modern translations of the Bible. When so many verses are either altered, questioned, or removed altogether, as in the NIV, nothing from then on, in the reader's mind, is certain. Not only does the whole Bible become suspect, but also all that its teachings were supposed to reinforce in his life are of less value to him now or shattered one by one.

First: His faith, that "cometh by hearing, and hearing by the word of God," has no sure anchor. The effect, FAITH, cannot exceed the cause, GOD'S WORD. Will not a defective Bible produce a defective faith?

Second: His obedience is compromised. A "thou shalt" or a "thou shalt not" loses both clarity and force on such an uncertain page. A nagging sin that might have been checked by a sure word from God is allowed to become more demanding than what forbids it. Until, finally, "the law of sin which is in (his) members," rather than the law of God, is obeyed.

Third: His worship and adoration is hindered. Since his love for God is based upon his estimation of God, here is where irreparable damage is done. Flawless Scriptures make Him a faultless God, while flawed Scriptures make Him an imperfect God. All of which offers the believer less to esteem, less to be awed by, less to love.

Fourth: His security is threatened. If God could not keep His Word forever, as He promised to do in Ps. 12:6, 7; Isa. 40:8; Matt. 24:35; 1 Pet. 1:25 and elsewhere, how will He keep the believer forever? What eternal hope, then, is left for him?

~ ~ ~ ~ ~ ~ ~ ~ ~ ~ ~ ~ ~

While all are entitled to every page of the Bible, no one has the right to meddle with its contents. To suggest that we must in order to repair certain passages that were supposedly damaged over the centuries, is to ignore the fact that the God Who produced the Bible did not abandon it to fate but has, Himself, promised to keep it. Again, "The words of the Lord are pure words:..Thou shalt keep them, O Lord, thou shalt preserve them from this generation for ever" (Ps. 12:6, 7).

Even if our faith balks at such a promise, surely we can believe that the God Who can lift us out of our fallen state and keep us as His Bride forever can preserve the pages of His own pure words over the brief passing of time.

If He could not keep the promise of Isa. 40:8: "the word of our God shall stand for ever," how will He keep the promise of John 3:36: "He that believeth on the Son hath everlasting life"?

~ ~ ~ ~ ~ ~ ~ ~ ~ ~ ~ ~

In summing up, let it be impressed upon our conscience that the success of any Christian movement will always be directly dependent upon its attitude toward Scripture. When the discipled are weak, it is because their ministers are weak. When the ministers are weak, it is because their denomination, theological schools, and resources are weak. When the denomination, theological schools, and resources are weak, it is because there is no longer any faith in the "inerrancy" of Scripture. This is a rather somber assessment, but since fellowships fall in precisely that manner, it is not difficult to see what lies just up ahead. Modern translations of the Bible with: (1) their glaringly different interpretations, (2) their own ideas of what should be retained of the Word of God and what should be left out, and (3) their impossible-to-ignore footnotes that shatter the faith of ministers and laymen alike, are moving the entire Christian movement of this century toward that hopeless end—a denial of INERRANCY by the Church universal. As we can witness already, the authority of Scripture and its Divine counsel are becoming less and less relevant to Christians. May God open our eyes before it is forever too late.

~ ~ ~ ~ ~ ~ ~ ~ ~ ~ ~ ~

Here, at the close of the book, is where writers generally attempt to make peace with those they have assailed. Where curt words are replaced with kind ones, apologies are made, and where something nice about their opponents is usually said so as not to leave the reader feeling that the peace that must be maintained in the Church has been broken. Yet, when an author attempts such appeasement, all that was accomplished through their research and efforts is nullified on the final page—to say nothing of leaving the reader a little less certain of just where to stand.

I have no apologies to offer for anything I have written. If I did, I should not have written it in the first place. Nor can I think of a kind thing to say about those who, in spite of all of the reasons not to, went ahead and gave to the English speaking world a Bible so immeasurably poor that the discerning cannot touch it.

If the Church cannot take a stand here and denounce such

attempts to destroy God's Word, it has no business denouncing anything at all. If it will not contend here, it should not contend anywhere.

Let me assure the reader that I have prepared this material prayerfully and with a clear conscience before God. If I did not and have intentionally taken up the wrong side of this issue, resisted God's Spirit, and done despite to the true Bible, then I deserve the severest chastisement at the hand of God. Of this, I am fully aware. Let the authors of the NIV and other modern translations now say the same. If they cannot, nor stand in complete confidence before God and His Church for the integrity of their work, then let them repent and make every effort to undo what they have done.

Dear reader, if the collective conscience of the Church does not admit soon to the seriousness of this matter its future, indeed, is bleak. If not for themselves, at least for their children, Christians must recognize that modern translations of the Bible are as traitorous to the "Written" Word, as Judas was to the "Living" Word and, therefore, deserve no honors but rather to be rebuked from every pulpit. It is impossible to conclude this matter in any other way.

~ ~ ~ ~ ~ ~ ~ ~ ~ ~ ~ ~

This book was not written to damage faith, create divisions, or to make this difficult matter more painful. Its purpose is to enlighten. In such a deceptive world, we need God's Bible and also to know that it is God's Bible. For only when we are thoroughly convinced that it is, will we cling, without questioning, to its flawless counsel. Then, as we feast on its contents, our soul will receive gladly the fullness of Christ, Who will not only master our lives but also lift us to heights of such holy excellence and intimacy with God as we could have hardly believed was possible.

Yes, how desperately we need God's Bible, and how relieved we should be to know that we have it. In spite of all of the attempts to destroy it, our God has kept His promise and preserved it to this hour. It is with us today in the time honored King James Version which continues to be the most quoted, memorized, and read (both publicly and privately) of all Bibles. The problems some claim to have overcoming its old English is more than made up for by its matchless beauty and accuracy.

Not only do English speaking Christians own in the King James Version the greatest translation of the Bible ever produced on earth, in any tongue, but also the greatest literary masterpiece the English language (or perhaps any language) has ever authored. Many believe it has no rival in the history of literature. "Its language," one said, "we reserve for God." Its power, sweep, and breathtaking authority transcend all other works, while its

Elizabethan eloquence, antiquated yet timeless, speaks more profoundly and intimately to our heart than our modern day tongue.

Indeed, no translation takes us closer to the Person and words of Jesus. One can feel the supernatural, the nearness of the Divine. As he goes from page to page, he has the literary experience of his life. The Bible becomes for the reader the BIBLE, not just a scrapbook of theological guesswork.

For nearly four centuries, innumerable saints have been instructed, comforted, and guided on their way, from sin through conversion to everlasting life, by this champion of all versions. Beyond question, in the King James Version, as in no other translation, can we grow in both the "grace, and in the KNOWLEDGE of our Lord and Saviour Jesus Christ."

The End

APPENDIX

Entirely aside from the intent of this book I would like here, in a few lines, to encourage the Christian.

As we are drawing closer (by the hour) to the return of Jesus, we should expect to find Christians anxiously working out their own salvation with fear and trembling. We also should expect them to be mindful of the times and to be ministering to as many as they possibly can. Yet, for the most part, the very opposite is true. Many of our brethren are slipping back into the world and, generally within the Church, there is a very placid outreach to others. What is more, we find too many Christians spending little or no time in prayer or the study of God's Word.

If you wish to live triumphantly you must keep uppermost in mind that Christ is your only hope; and that every bit of you and what is yours must be built into and around Him. Jesus must never be just a part of your life: He must be the One Who rules over and sustains every bit of it. As your God and Creator, He must be your All—the One you live for today and will die for tomorrow.

Acknowledge that before you are anything else in this life you are a Christian and, as such, your first responsibility is to please Jesus. Therefore, above all things, LOVE JESUS SUPREMELY. In total surrender, give Him every bit of your life. And, as you lean daily upon His strength, put ALL OF YOUR FAITH IN HIM. He alone saved you; and He alone can keep you saved.

Realize that before you are to minister to anyone you must first minister to God. You accomplish this through prayer, praise, worship, obedience, and by both studying and employing His Word. Remember, you are the Bride of Jesus. As such, your greatest responsibility in this life is to maintain, with the uttermost care, your relationship with Him. If Jesus is not everything to you, you will not convince others that He can be everything to them.

Reach out to as many as you possibly can, in this life. Love them with all of your heart; and pray for them without ceasing. Be concerned, most of all, for their spiritual lives. Pray, that when this life is over, they may escape Hell's fire and enter with you into God's glorious rest.

If you are a discouraged pastor because your people are not committed to you, church attendance, or tithing, the reason for this is: they are not committed to Christ. We, in the ministry, have been trying for too long to get more out of people's lives than what Christ can get out of them. There is only one solution. Turn them over to Christ. Get rid of everything you are using to make Christianity attractive. While such novelties entice the flesh they do nothing for the soul. Preach for commitment! Aim for the heart! Require, as God does, repentance and total surrender to Jesus.

May God bless you richly forever.

If you are not a Christian, please read carefully what my wife has to say in the following:

Dear reader:

Can you remember ever asking Jesus Christ to come into your heart? If you cannot, Jesus welcomes you to do that right now!

Jesus said, "Come unto me, all ye that labour and are heavy laden, and I will give you rest" (Matt. 11:28). This beautiful verse of Scripture assures us that Jesus is a refuge. If you come to Christ, and fully receive Him, you will have this rest that He promises to give. The rest, peace, and pardon that Christ gives is genuine and can only be obtained through Him.

Most importantly, Jesus offers you eternal life. The Bible tells us that Jesus Himself, is "Eternal Life." Therefore, when you receive Jesus as your Saviour you are receiving eternal life! The Bible says, "For the wages of sin is death; but the gift of God is eternal life through Jesus Christ our Lord" (Rom. 6:23). "And this is the record, that God hath given to us eternal life, and this life is in his Son" (I John 5:11).

The Apostle Paul wrote: "That he (God the Father) would grant you, according to the riches of his glory, to be strengthened with might by his Spirit in the inner man; **That Christ may dwell in your hearts by faith**; that ye, being rooted and grounded in love, May be able to comprehend with all saints what is the breadth, and length, and depth, and height; And to know the love of Christ, which passeth knowledge, that ye might be filled with all the fulness of God" (Eph. 3:16-19). This is truly magnificent! Jesus Christ actually dwells in the hearts of those who come to Him for Salvation.

God offers His love and salvation to you but it will require participation on your part. You must come to Christ with a truly surrendered heart; and then give yourself completely to Him. If you are willing to ask Jesus Christ to come into your life, please pray:

1.) Jesus, I do believe that You are the true Son of God, Who came in the flesh, and that You died on the cross for me.

2.) I believe that You want to save me. Therefore, I put all of my faith in You.

3.) Jesus, I admit that I am a sinner. I know the Blood that You shed on the cross made an atonement for my sins. You paid my debt in full! Please forgive me for all of my sins. Jesus, I need You. I want to live my life for You. Come into my heart right now and be my Lord and Saviour. Thank You, Lord Jesus, for saving my soul.

If you have said this prayer, inviting Jesus into your life, you can be very sure that He has answered your prayer. You are Born Again! You have entered into a new life! "Therefore if any man be in Christ, he is a new creature: old things are passed away; behold, all things are become new" (2 Cor. 5:17).

Jesus says, "Behold, I stand at the door, and knock: if any man hear my voice, and open the door, I will come in to him, and will sup with him, and he with me" (Rev. 3:20). The moment you opened your heart to Christ, and received Him as your Lord and Saviour, you began to have fellowship with Him. A great change has already taken place in you. You may feel it; you may not. Put your trust in God that this change has taken place. Let joy begin to fill your heart. CHRIST HAS SAVED YOU! Rejoice now and always in this!

The Holy Spirit will give you guidance and Spiritual discernment as He works within your life. He will build you up in Christ through His Spiritual Fruits and Gifts. The Holy Spirit will always glorify Jesus; therefore, your life also should glorify Jesus. There is always perfect unity between the Father, the Son, and the Holy Spirit. They will work in you and enable you to live a holy life.

As you begin living the Christian life, your family and friends will notice the change that has taken place in you. God is concerned about their need for salvation as well. Make sure you tell them that Jesus wants to love and save them too.

Now that you are a Christian it will be necessary to find a good church. Pray that God will direct you in this matter. When you find a good church be sure that you attend it faithfully.

This is very important: Be sure that Christ is in the center of everything that surrounds your life. You should live in a way that fully pleases Him. Be sure that you Love God with all of your heart. Make it your habit to pray and read your Bible every day. Your heart will be blessed, and at peace with God, when you do these things.

I pray that our wonderful Lord will abundantly keep you in His Grace, Strength, Peace, and Love.

In the love of Jesus Christ,
Maureen Salliby

NOTES

[1] Streeter, *The Four Gospels*, 1930, p. 30.

[2] Scrivener, *Introduction to New Testament Criticism*, 3rd Edition, p. 311. (Published by the Bible For Today, Inc., 900 Park Ave., Collingswood, NJ 08108, BFT # 1285.)

[3] Eusebius, *Ecclesiastical History*, LCS, Vol. I, pp. 522-524.

[4] McClintock and Strong, *Cyclopedia*, Vol. VII, p. 430.

[5] Westcott, *Life of Westcott*, Vol. II, p. 69.

[6] Hort, *Life of Hort*, Vol. II, p. 50.

[7] Westcott, *Life of Westcott*, Vol. I, p. 81.

[8] Westcott, *Life of Westcott*, Vol. II, p. 50.

[9] Hort, *Life of Hort*, Vol. I, p. 400.

[10] Hort, *Life of Hort*, Vol. II, p. 86.

[11] Hort, *Life of Hort*, Vol. II, p. 51.

[12] Hort, *Life of Hort*, Vol. I, p. 76.

[13] Hort, *Life of Hort*, Vol. II, p. 30.

[14] Hort, *Life of Hort*, Vol. I, p. 76.

[15] Hort, *Life of Hort*, Vol. I, p. 430.

[16] Pickering, *John William Burgon And The New Testament*, Part II

[17] Burgon, *The Revision Revised*, p. 293

INDEX OF VERSE COMPARISON SCRIPTURES

	Item #		Item #
Mic. 5:2	19	Luke 1:28	41
		Luke 2:14	65
Matt. 1:25	42	Luke 2:33	39
Matt. 5:22	84	Luke 2:43	40
Matt. 5:44	66	Luke 2:49	51
Matt. 6:13	110	Luke 4:4	72
Matt. 6:27	86	Luke 4:8	84
Matt. 8:2	48	Luke 4:18	62
Matt. 9:13	3	Luke 4:44	94
Matt. 9:18	47	Luke 6:48	92
Matt. 11:19	88	Luke 8:43	54
Matt. 15:6	84	Luke 8:48	63
Matt. 15:8	84	Luke 9:7	59
Matt. 16:20	155	Luke 9:55	73
Matt. 17:21	107	Luke 9:56	1
Matt. 18:11	2	Luke 9:62	93
Matt. 18:22	85	Luke 10:15	99
Matt. 19:9	84	Luke 10:19	64
Matt. 19:17	89	Luke 11:2	109
Matt. 20:7	84	Luke 11:11	84
Matt. 20:16	68	Luke 11:41	94
Matt. 20:22	113	Luke 11:54	112
Matt. 23:8	136	Luke 14:5	87
Matt. 23:10	137	Luke 20:23	75
Matt. 23:14	70	Luke 22:64	116
Matt. 24:7	84	Luke 22:68	117
Matt. 24:36	36	Luke 23:15	118
Matt. 25:13	145	Luke 23:17	119
Matt. 25:31	132	Luke 23:23	121
Matt. 27:24	122	Luke 23:38	125
Matt. 27:35	124	Luke 24:1	128
		Luke 24:42	129
Mark 1:31	56		
Mark 3:15	61	John 1:27	37
Mark 3:29	100	John 3:13	46
Mark 6:11	69	John 3:15	98
Mark 6:33	60	John 5:4	53
Mark 6:51	58	John 5:16	111
Mark 7:8	84	John 6:11	57
Mark 7:16	74	John 6:47	12
Mark 8:26	84	John 6:69	38
Mark 9:29	106	John 8:9	77
Mark 9:44	96	John 8:35	147
Mark 9:45	95	John 9:4	50
Mark 9:46	97	John 9:35	33
Mark 9:49	84	John 11:41	55
Mark 10:21	84	John 13:23	114
Mark 10:24	71	John 14:2	90
Mark 11:26	67	John 16:16	130
Mark 13:14	84	John 17:5	131
Mark 13:33	105	John 18:40	120
Mark 14:24	91		
Mark 15:28	123	Acts 2:27	126

	Item #		Item #
Acts 2:30	44	1 Tim. 3:16	20
Acts 2:31	127	1 Tim. 6:5	78
Acts 3:13	34	1 Tim. 6:14,15	139
Acts 3:26	35		
Acts 7:37	52	Heb. 3:6	138
Acts 8:37	4	Heb. 7:21	134
Acts 9:5,6	5	Heb. 9:11	94
Acts 10:30	108	Heb. 10:30	29
Acts 15:18	26		
Acts 15:18	49	1 Pet. 3:15	24
Acts 23:9	76	1 Pet. 4:1	13
Acts 28:29	18	1 Pet. 4:14	133
Rom. 1:16	11	2 Pet. 2:17	101
Rom. 10:15	82	2 Pet. 3:10	104
Rom. 11:6	144		
Rom. 14:10-12	27	1 John 4:3	45
Rom. 14:21	81	1 John 5:7,8	23
Rom. 16:24	143	1 John 5:13	15
1 Cor. 5:7	14	2 John 9	152
1 Cor. 9:18	10		
1 Cor. 10:28	135	Jude 25	25
1 Cor. 11:24	115		
1 Cor. 15:47	151	Rev. 1:8	148
		Rev. 1:8-13	22
2 Cor. 2:17	83	Rev. 1:11	149
		Rev. 2:13	84
Gal. 3:1	80	Rev. 5:10	94
Gal. 3:17	9	Rev. 5:14	150
Gal. 4:7	8	Rev. 8:13	94
Gal. 6:15	7	Rev. 11:17	146
		Rev. 13:1	94
Eph. 3:9	31	Rev. 14:5	30
Eph. 3:14	32	Rev. 20:12	28
Eph. 4:6	16	Rev. 21:24	17
Eph. 5:9	94	Rev. 22:14	94
Eph. 5:30	43		
Phil. 2:5,6	21		
Phil. 3:16	79		
Phil. 4:13	154		
Col. 1:2	141		
Col. 1:14	6		
Col. 3:6	103		
Col. 4:8	94		
Col. 4:15	94		
1 Thess. 1:1	142		
1 Thess. 2:16	102		
1 Tim. 2:7	153		